JUST A LITTLE PRICK
My Nursing Life

Carol Bissett

Published in 2020 by Carol Bissett

© Copyright Carol Bissett

ISBN: 978-1-9162758-4-3

Printed in the UK by INGRAM

Book & Cover Design by Russell Holden

www.pixeltweakspublications.com

Nurse icon courtesy of Freepik
A Catalogue record for this book is available from the British Library.

Printed by Ingram

Foreword

During my nursing career I worked in many hospitals, in different locations and for different health authorities. During this time, I was privileged to work with some wonderful people and look after many patience who's lives, and deaths have help shape me into the person I am today.

This book is a snapshot of my nursing career, most of which I thoroughly enjoyed. However, there were times that this profession took its toll on me.

Saying that I wouldn't have wanted it any other way.

All stories are true though the timeline maybe a little skewed, but the names I have used are fictitious, apart from one or two.

The NHS is a wonderful institution for which we should all be grateful, but I fear for its health and well-being in years to come.

Lots of things have changed while I have been nursing. Some good, some bad.

We have made fabulous advances in medical science. We can keep people alive longer, we can treat people who in the past would have certainly died. However somewhere here we lost the essence of good nursing care and practical qualifications.

There are without doubt truly dedicated nurses and doctors out there, and maybe we expect too much these days. Power is knowledge. The patient of today can access and research their condition and treatment.

Do we then, at times expect the impossible?

Acknowledgements

I would like to thank my beta readers Lesley Graves, Elizabeth McGuire, Maggie Montague and Jane Morphet for their time and their honest opinions.

I would also like to thank my editor, Liz Hedgecock for her work, helping me make this book a better read.

Russ, at Pixel Tweaks Publications, again for his magic enabling these words to take the form of a real book.

To him in doors. Always there for me in everything I do.

Any finally to all the dedicated nurses out there, without you we would be at a loss. You are the stars in the darkest of nights.

For Joan Hartley.

A good friend

A good colleague

And a bloody brilliant nurse!

PART ONE
1969-1971

Chapter 1

Now

'So, what else can cause anaphylactic shock?' I asked a room of twenty students who looked somewhat bored with the information I was trying to impart into their knowledge base. At the very least I hope that the training I was delivering would stop them from killing someone. 'Eggs?' asked a student who, unlike the rest, seemed to be engaging with me and had a smile on her face. The optimistic part of me thought how gratifying it was to have such an eager student, but the pessimistic side of my personality was wondering what drugs she was on, and whether she had any to spare.

'Yes, eggs can be a vaccinator's nightmare. Good answer. But in truth, we can develop a severe reaction to almost anything. I remember when I did a stint on A&E, a woman came in with life-threatening anaphylaxis. She was treated successfully, and we discovered eventually that she was allergic to the condom her partner had used. So much for safe sex!'

This had their attention again, and I even got a little titter. Nothing like sex, or stories about stupid people, to lighten the situation in a dull lecture theatre, and I had many such tales to tell.

The day finally ended, and as people escaped into the daylight I packed up my equipment and wondered if it might be time for me to put away my nursing career as well.

The NHS now demanded even more paperwork and stress for already overworked, underpaid nurses, in that we had to do something called 'revalidation'. (Since 2016 qualified nurses in the UK have to demonstrate that they are safe to practice. This has to be done every three years).

I was 62; did I really have to prove to some nameless twonk in London that I could do my job? Don't get me wrong, I'm all for a tight ship being run after Shipman, (sorry about the pun) and we need to make sure our medical staff know what they are doing. That was my job, when it came to vaccinations, so what did I have to prove?

I think that this decision by the Department of Health was one of the worse ones they ever made, as far as the nursing profession was concerned, and they have made some corkers over the years. All revalidation did was create a mass exodus of nurses of a certain age, retiring because they didn't want to jump through more hoops, when they had intended to carry on because they loved their work, they needed to work, or they just weren't ready to go.

Since I finally made my decision to leave, I have had countless emails from the NMC (the Nursing and Midwifery Council) asking me to do a 'back to work course' because guess what, they are short of nurses and very, very short of experienced nurses.

I wonder if someone has correlated the two events, but I doubt it. And even if they have, no one is ever going to admit it and say 'well, we got that wrong!' I like to think I had come a long way in my years as a nurse, but in truth, I was just pulled along with the changing face of the NHS. It had always manipulated its staff to a greater or lesser degree, and the doctrine of change in the name of progress isn't always the right thing to do. But that's just my opinion.

Chapter 2

1969

'What do you mean, you've got a pain in your belly and your bum won't work?'

This was an expression I hadn't heard before, but as the person telling me this was a five-year-old who had just had his tonsils out, I doubt it was a term you would find in many medical books.

It was my first day on ENT (Ear Nose & Throat) at a North West children's hospital. No, let's get this straight, it was my first day in nursing, full stop. I'm not sure who was the most terrified, the five-year-old who couldn't poo, or me that couldn't stop.! But like most wounded animals he saw in me another frightened soul, and thought I wouldn't make him eat cornflakes while his throat was still red, sore and he felt sick.

I kid you not. Day three, cornflakes for breakfast. It was like asking them to eat razor blades. Of course no one ate them, and if they tried, the cornflakes all ended up in the same place; in the bucket. I was told that this was part of the healing process. Really? Ice cream and jelly was about as much as the poor little mites could manage, and I just thought it cruel to try and force them to eat anything else.

But these were those days when after two bouts of tonsillitis your GP sent you off to the hospital and they whipped out those little balls of fun. Someone needed to say that they are important, and part of our lymphatic system which tries to stop an infection before it gets a real hold on our bodies. You would think all those clever bods who did a five-year medical degree would know this, wouldn't you? However, if your next-door neighbour's son had been through this little horror story, why shouldn't your child?

To be fair we trusted doctors then much more than we do now, and would take their advice blindly, so I'm being slightly unfair to say that it was a trend. No, to hell with it. It was a trend!

And, you may ask, how did I get to this point? A very good question.

I was manoeuvred into training as a nurse by a very clever careers advisor. She had a remit to fill the courses at the new technical college in my town. Because of this I started down a road that had many pauses, turns and pit stops, just because my best subject at school happened to be biology. The college provided an entrance route for wannabee nurses. Well, why not!

I enjoyed the pre-nursing course very much and left with a reasonable amount of GCE 'O Levels.' (yes, I'm that old), so I applied to do a cadetship at the afore mentioned hospital as I wanted to be a children's nurse, or so I thought at the time. Also, I had to live in the nurses' home, as it was too far to travel each day, and this was the most exciting part of the adventure for me.

What I hadn't bargained for was the fact that on day two the most horrendous homesickness hit me as a bolt from the blue. It was something I hadn't even considered, and I think perhaps the nurses' home might have had something to do with it.

My cell, oops sorry, my room was a stark little box with a single bed, a wardrobe, a bedside table with a lamp on it and a rug on the wooden floor. There was a sink in the corner and a window that would only open about four inches. This was to stop anyone (men) climbing in or out, apparently.

As my room was on the second floor, and there was a sheer drop from the window of about thirty feet, I didn't think that was very likely. What did bother me slightly was the fact that I could burn to death because of the window situation, but at least I would die a virgin.

I didn't sleep the first night because of the screams of my neighbours, who had foolishly opened their doors to friendly knocks and had then been dragged out of their rooms and dumped fully-clothed in cold baths. It was some sort of initiation ceremony. Oh, how we laughed. But I locked myself in and lay trembling in the dark, ignoring the hammering on my door at 2 a.m. So missed that little joy.

The actual ENT ward I was allocated to was okay. The staff were nice, the patients cute, and I was having fun playing with the children, until the sister spoilt it by telling me some bandages needed washing in the bathroom.

I was shown a massive bag full of dirty crepe bandages and instructed to half-fill the bath with antiseptic liquid and hot water, wash the bandages through, rinse them and then put them on an airer over the bath to dry.

Just think of the money we could save if we still did this? No? No. Even then I thought it slightly unhygienic. And why in God's name did an ENT ward need so many bandages?

I never did find out because I managed four days at this hospital and then I left. I somehow found the courage to march into the matron's office on Thursday of my first week and declare to her that I couldn't spend another night in that prison they had the gall to call home.

'Last night,' I told her while I was on a roll, 'I heard someone shout down each corridor that whoever had stolen her knickers from the laundry room had better put them back, otherwise, they would catch what she had. And this morning the cleaner let herself into my room and shouted in my face "Get up!"'

'It does take some getting used to,' she admitted. 'If you decide to come back at eighteen to start your training properly, we will gladly have you.' I must admit she was very kind, but also well-practiced in this sort of confrontation.

I ran back to my room, packed my case, and as I got to the front door bumped into the home sister. This is the lady, usually a trained nurse, who looks after the nurses living in. She was to be feared and what she said was law. 'Where do you think you're going, young lady?'

'Home.'

'This is your home now.'

'Like fuck it is,' I said as I ran for the hills.

Chapter 3

What Now?

Some say it's not what you know, but who you know that gets you a place in life, and this was certainly true of my next nursing job.

I went home with my tail between my legs, and wouldn't go out for a week. Then I called to see my old college tutor, confessing my failure. I'm not sure why, but doing this made things seem better, a bit like going to see the local priest and telling him all your mortal sins, I suppose. She was a very wise woman and didn't think I was stupid or a coward at all. 'I cried every night for three months when I first left home to train to be a nurse and lost 2 stone in weight.' She also said that at least I had the good common sense to get out quickly and therefore, if I wanted her to, she could make a few phone calls and see if she could get me in at the local hospital, so that I could live at home and travel into work each day.

Two weeks later saw me starting at my second job in less than a month, this time at a general hospital, and just a half-hour bus ride away from all that I knew and loved.

They put me on casualty for my first placement. This will be interesting, I thought. I'll see some exciting things here. But no. Unless you consider cleaning the toilets and hand basins in the department's facilities as interesting, or folding up laundry and stacking it in the linen cupboard as educational. If I was really lucky I got to deliver prescriptions to the pharmacy, or if I was really, really lucky, showing a relative up to the ward where their sick or injured family member was being looked after.

But I kept my head down and got on with the job, at least until the senior sister returned to the department. She had been on some sort of extended leave during my first four weeks of working on casualty, and it was hatred at first sight. To this day I still don't know why, but she made my life a misery from the moment she laid eyes on me. She shouted at me, told me I was no good at the jobs I was given, and generally bullied me. If she had treated everyone the same way it wouldn't have seemed as bad, but she was at least civil to most of her staff.

I put up with it and just tried to keep out of her way, but she had some sort of super-sense of where I was and always managed to rout me out.

The last straw was the day she sent me into the toilets to clean them, which I did, and then came to check my work. She looked around and wasn't satisfied at all with my efforts. 'Do it again, nurse,' she said without giving me any eye contact. 'But it's the end of my shift.' That was the wrong thing to say. She came very close to me and hissed, 'You can go when I say you can go. Now do it again!'

There was no point in even trying to argue. I couldn't win. The fact that I would miss my bus and end up getting home almost two hours late was not her concern. I did it again. And when I went to find the sadist, I was calmly told she had gone off duty half an hour before.

As I got home my mother was on the point of calling the police, convinced I'd been murdered. We didn't have a phone so there was no way of letting her know that I was going to be so late. Say what you like about mobile phones, they are bloody handy.

When my mum asked me why I was this late my stiff upper lip wilted slightly, and it all came pouring out. Until then I hadn't said what I was going through at work to anyone, as I didn't want people to think I was so pathetic that I just couldn't hack it, again.

The next day when I woke up at ten o'clock, I panicked. Jumping out of bed the fear running down my spine at the way my 'no show' at work would be viewed, and more to the point, how many toilets I would have to clean to make up for it.

I rushed downstairs to find my dad with a cup of tea waiting for me. 'Where's Mum? Why didn't she wake me? I'm going to get into so much trouble for this!' The words came tumbling out.

'Sit down and drink this. You're not going into work today.'

'What? What do you mean?'

'Your mum will explain when she gets back.'

'Back from where?'

'Hospital.' Dad was a man of few words.

'The hospital? Is she ill? Which hospital?' I was obviously still asleep, and this was some sort of bizarre dream.

'Your hospital.' He sipped his tea calmly.

'What for?'

'She's gone to sort that woman out.'

'What woman?'

'That sister. That bully, more like it.' Now there was an edge to his voice. He was trying hard to keep a lid on his anger,

'What! She can't do that.'

'Oh, I think she can, love. Now drink that tea before it gets cold.'

Chapter 4

Meanwhile, back at the Hospital

My mum was the gentlest person you could ever wish to meet. I never heard her say a bad word about anyone, but where her children were concerned she channelled the lioness in her that all mothers have.

I'll never really knew what went on that day, however. I was off work with stress for two weeks and when I went back, I had been moved to a new department.

The matron even sent for me on my first day back to ask if I was feeling better. She didn't refer to the reason I had been off, or the fact that she had moved me, something that hardly ever happened. We didn't complain in those days; we didn't have any rights. We just got on with it.

The rest of my time as a cadet was uneventful and sometimes even fun, and my favourite placement wasn't a ward, it was my next one after 'Casualty gate'; the pharmacy.

Here there were a lot of smiling faces and plenty of laughter. After what I had been through I realised that this was a very relaxed atmosphere, but the work still got done, and done efficiently.

They didn't even have a go at me when I dropped a crate of twelve bottles of the antiseptic solution Cetrimide one day, managing to break four of them. I was presented with a mop and bucket and told that accidents happen.

What they didn't tell me was that the solution was very soapy and once the mopping began so did the growth of soapsuds and bubbles. It took me over an hour to clean up the mess I'd made, and about six changes of water in the bucket, but I must say the floor and surrounding area were extremely clean, and not one germ could have possibly survived the Cetrimide holocaust that I inflicted upon them. And now I knew where that 'hospital' smell came from.

As the year sped onwards, talk began about the next intake to PTS (Preliminary Training School) in September, the set that I was due to enter. This again would mean leaving home, for the first twelve weeks at least.

The rule at this hospital, and I think it was a general way of doing things, was that a student nurse had to live in for the first twelve weeks of the training programme. This applied even to married women, but not to men. One, because very few men trained to be nurses back in the 1960s and two, there would have been the problem of where to put them. After all, they were bound to be sex fiends and have their wicked way with all the female students. No? Well, one can dream.

It was also very unusual for the training school to accept married women. But we had a few anomalies that September. There was a married woman in our set, and two men. But the most unusual person was a Chinese nursing student. Such exotic colleagues were very seldom seen in the North West of England. She had been doing her two-year course in London to become an enrolled nurse and now was doing another two years to convert to full registration. She was tiny with a very small 't', spoke English so well that she put the rest of us to shame, but the thing I remember most about her was her 16-inch waist. She was like a doll.

This time leaving home held no terrors for me. I knew five of the girls I was to train with as we had all been cadets together, and I was only a bus ride away if I wanted to nip home. Also, at the end of the twelve weeks, if I passed my first exam, I had the option to either live out or stay at the nurses' home, so because I didn't have to make too many long-term decisions at once it was all much easier to accept.

For the second time I was moving away from home. I was filled with confidence and looking forward to becoming a real nurse. My parents were proud of me, even though my dad wanted me to go into the police force. Why? Because I was tall. Not the best reason to go into law enforcement I know. But nursing was going to be my future. I was going to save lives and make sick people better.

If only I had known then what I know now!

Chapter 5

So let us begin

Our uniform was the same as that of a cadet nurse, a white fitted overall. However, and this makes all the difference, we were allowed to wear a nurse's cap. Presented with two pieces of what looked like starched cardboard (later I was to wear actual cardboard on my head), we all spent a happy half-hour before the first lecture trying to get the cap to exactly the right shape. Once it had been moulded to fit your head and cover your hair, that cap was looked after like a newborn baby until the day when it had to go back to the laundry to be turned into a flat pack again, and you just knew your next cap would never be as good.

There were 30 of us in September set 1970, and this was about the average size of most intakes.

The expected drop-out rate was about 30% before the 3-year training programme came to an end, and usually a few of those drop outs happened before the end of PTS.

As we all sat there in the School of Nursing on our first day, with white uniforms and bright eager faces, we didn't know what to expect. Two sister tutors came into the room and we all stood until we were told 'Sit down please, nurses.' Now that was a shock, the 'please' I mean. I wasn't used to sisters being nice; or not to me, at least. But I was about to have a delightful experience. Not one, but both of the tutors in front of the class appeared happy, cheerful and gentle. I wouldn't have wanted to test their congeniality too much, but I felt myself relax, and I enjoyed the tasks that were given to us.

We were taught in our first week how to make beds (I could do that), how to do bed-baths (I could do that), and how to give an enema (I did not want to do that!). There was also a lot of theory, and I mean a lot, so most evenings were spent either in the common room or in our bedrooms, studying.

On the flip side we had every weekend off, and that meant I could go home on Friday evening and come back on Sunday. Not Monday morning, it had to be Sunday before 10 pm, as at that time the doors to the nurses' home were firmly locked and bolted. Sneaking in was like running the gauntlet, because if home sister caught you that was a black mark against your record, and no one wanted that.

As a group we gelled quickly, and I can't remember anyone not getting on. Maybe that's because we were all in the same boat, and even the ones that had been cadets felt the pressure, in some ways more. Most of the newbies were brain-boxes and handled the academic side of our course without too much stress, but those among us who weren't that clever had to study very hard, so knowing the hospital, where to have a sneaky fag, or how to get out of the doctors' residence without being seen wasn't that much help at this point in our careers. Take Pam for instance. She had four A levels. She was ex-grammar school and her teachers had been horrified that she wanted to do such a lowly job as nursing when she could be a teacher. Yes, really. However, she was lovely, and we became friends. We would get the bus home together on a Friday, and after a few weeks I even got offered a lift back in her dad's car on a Sunday evening. That meant a few more hours at home, as the Sunday bus service was unpredictable, to say the least. She became an excellent nurse, despite her teachers' 'higher' aspirations for her!

Then there was Mary. She had come across from Northern Ireland and suffered from the same homesickness I had had when I first left home. I could empathise with her, and she would come into my room after her evening phone call home and cry on my shoulder. I would provide sympathy, tissues, and hot sweet tea, and hope that made her feel just a bit better.

The twelve weeks flew by and the last week found us cramming for our end-of-block exam. To fail would mean a review with sister tutor to see if you were up to the training, which was only going to get harder. Therefore if you couldn't pass this exam you usually got asked to reconsider your career choices (asked to leave). Even though we were told this seldom occurred, we all panicked, presuming that it was bound to happen to us.

Our statistical representative for not making it to the end of the first 12 weeks was Susan, someone that I had been a cadet with. She was very beautiful, full of good humour and compassion, and she was pregnant.

She had suspected this when she started in PTS, but four weeks in she had it confirmed and said a fond farewell to us. I asked her how she felt, and she said 'Wonderful. I'm having the baby of a boy I loved very much, and we are getting married in six weeks.'

Susan's mum and dad were giving up rooms of their home for the new little family until they could afford a place of their own. It did appear, at eighteen years old, she had it sorted. In a way I envied her. She was so content with her lot.

It was just before we finished PTS for two weeks' holiday that we heard she had lost the baby. We all felt for her and wondered if she would come back into nursing, but as far as I know she didn't. I often thought of Susan. Was she happy? How did things turn out for her? I also took the saying 'Be careful what you wish for' as a mantra for life.

The entire group passed; collective sigh of relief! And as we packed for two whole weeks' holiday, we all felt like we were walking on air.

I had been asked if I wanted to stay at the nurses' home, and said that I did, so I would be 'upgraded' on my return. Our last job before we went home was to go to our allocated wards and pick up our off duty (nurses work rota) for our return. We had all been introduced to our new working environment during PTS, but only very briefly.

I was to be on women's medical with another nurse from our set, and it seemed all right from the outside. One girl had worked on there as a cadet and said the senior sister was firm but fair, and that would do for me.

As I waited for a lift in my friend's father's car, we saw Mary jump into a taxi to take her to the airport. She was going home for the first time since we started training, and was very excited. 'See you in two weeks!', she shouted.

We looked at each other and both said at the same time, 'She won't be back!'

Chapter 6

Different uniform, same shit!

No hiding now. I was in the uniform of a student nurse, proper apron and everything.

I collected my work clothes from the sewing room on my first day back and I was presented with two dresses and two aprons (I already had the caps). We wore one dress and one apron for five and a half days, as we only got one and a half days off for 3 weeks of the month, and once a month we got two whole days, together if we were lucky.

We had been measured up while still in PTS, and the go-ahead to alter our uniforms from brand new or, more usually, second hand, was given to the sewing room once we had passed our exam. I've got to say they fitted like a glove, and I did feel different when I put it on, a bit like Spiderman in his costume. I had superpowers now.

First day on the ward I was a bundle of nerves, I hadn't slept well, and I was running on adrenaline. All the nursing staff gathered in the sister's office for the report and then we had to check the workbook to see what jobs we had been allocated for the shift.

I was working with an enrolled nurse and we were going to do beds. This meant each patient got a lick with a facecloth and their bed made up with clean linen. Yes, it was more important that the beds were cleaner than the patients.

The enrolled nurse was a sulky woman and didn't smile at all during my time on that ward. She was abrupt with the staff (except for sister, whom I think she was in love with), and more worryingly, the patients.

The first bed we went to had the warning smell of something foul. Sure enough, Mrs Smith was, to put it nicely, in a bit of a mess. The mess extended from her little toes to her left armpit.

'Oh, dear God. You dirty woman. Why didn't you ask someone for a bedpan?'

I wasn't expecting that response and must have looked shocked, but the EN didn't miss a beat.

'Right.' She went into action and had the woman sat in an armchair on an already dirty sheet, stripped the bed, and told me to go and run a bath. We whisked said lady to the bathroom and had her smelling like a rose and firmly pinned in bed by hospital corners before you could say 'Where there's muck there's money.'

Even though the EN was rough of tongue, she was very gentle physically with the patient, which made for an odd working methodology. I didn't mind being paired with her, even with her brisk attitude, as she got things done, and I did learn a lot with her guidance.

Three episodes stick in my mind from my time on that ward, and the first was an encounter with a nun who was also a qualified nurse. We had two working alongside us on this woman's medical ward from the local convent. They were both waiting to go and do God's work in another country, and they were diligent, hardworking and kind to all the little old ladies, so I was surprised one day to find one of these angels of mercy having a real go at a young patient.

'You will only know eternal damnation, and you will burn in hell for what you've done.'

She came from behind the curtains leaving the poor woman in bits. I waited until she had gone into a side ward and sneaked in to see if I could calm the woman down.

'Whatever is the matter?' I asked as I took in the swollen, blotchy eyes.

'I've done a terrible thing.'

'It can't be that bad.'

'Yes. Yes, it is. I killed my baby.'

Ah, now it began to make sense. It transpired that the poor woman had been forced to have a termination by her husband because the baby wasn't his. It was all legal and above board, but she hadn't needed the religious input as she felt bad enough anyway. The only reason she was with us was that she had developed an infection and needed intrarmuscular antibiotics.

When I voiced my concerns to our ward sister, she told me I didn't know what I was talking about, and to just do what I was told.

I never learn, do I? My opinion as a very new student nurse only put me on the naughty step with my superior. Nurses did not ask why we did things then, we just did what we were told, apparently!

The second event was when a lovely lady was admitted with an acute episode of MS. (Multiple Sclerosis.)

She was very ill when she came in, but made steady progress, and I formed that forbidden thing, a friendship, with her. She was only in her mid-thirties, and that made her, as a long stay patient, as close to my age as I was likely to get on this ward.

One night her husband didn't come to visit, which was unusual. I brought the portable phone after everyone had gone, but she got no answer when she called her home number.

The next night no show again, then ten minutes before visiting time was over a middle-aged woman came to see my friend/patient. She sat down at the side of her bed and took her hand. Whatever she was telling her was obviously bad news, but I didn't get a chance to speak to her until I was due to go off duty about an hour later.

'Are you okay?' I asked, though it wouldn't take a degree in psychology to see that she was far from okay.

'He's left me.'

'Who?'

'My husband, he's packed his bags and gone.'

'Gone where?' I sat down with a thump on the end of the bed, finding it almost impossible to believe her loving husband had deserted her. 'He's been having an affair for about six months, but I didn't think...'

'What a complete bastard.' It just came out.

'No, he's not. He's loving and caring, but he's just had enough. I don't blame him.' And she meant it.

Two weeks later she was discharged to a nursing home. That was the first time I cried over a patient, but it wasn't the last time.

And finally, Ethel.

I met Ethel during my first week on the ward. She was 88, very cantankerous, and we all developed temporary deafness when she got too much. She was admitted for a week every three months or so, to give her long-suffering son and daughter-in-law respite. Ethel could test the patience of a saint; even the nuns avoided her.

It was my last few days on women's medical when Ethel came to visit us again. I just counted my lucky stars that I wouldn't be there for her full stay.

The EN and I had got her settled for visiting, and it started. 'No one will visit me of course, I'm not worth a visit.'

'But Ethel, you're here so your relatives can have a holiday.' I pointed out.

'It's fine for them, swanning off and leaving me in this hell hole to die.'

'Don't be so selfish, you miserable old woman. Of course you're not going to die,' the EN said to her sternly.

'Wasn't that a bit mean?' I asked with a smile as we walked away.

'No, it was the truth,' the EN said emphatically.

As the evening wore on, Ethel upped the ante. 'Nurse, can you just plump up my pillow? Nurse, can you pour me out some water? Nurse, can you sit me up? Nurse, can you lay me down? That's too much! That's not enough! Nurse, can you move that wall a bit to the right?' No, she didn't say that, but it wouldn't have surprised me if she had.

'Nurse, could I have a little more sugar in my tea please?' This was to me, so I put another bit of sugar in her cup. She sipped it and then pulled a face. 'That's too sweet now. Can I have a fresh cup?'

'No Ethel, not just now, I'm busy.'

'Oh well, if you're too busy to help a dying woman...'

I had had enough. 'Ethel, you are as strong as a horse. You are not dying. You have nothing wrong with you except old age. Now stop complaining.' And I stomped off, feeling that Ethel's relatives deserved a huge gold medal for the care they gave to this very demanding woman.

I finally got back to my room forty minutes late, mostly due to Ethel. I flopped on my bed and sighed, knowing that this time tomorrow I would be at home with my mum looking after me.

I slept well that night, as I did most nights. I think it's known as exhaustion.

The next morning, I went onto the ward ready to do that last shift and then move on.

We all settled in the office for the report. Sister looked slightly more serious than usual and then she came out with it. 'Ethel died last night.' We all looked at each other, and I suspect every one of us felt awful, since not one of us had a nice word to say to her the night before.

Then the EN did what she did best, spoke her mind. 'The Lord is good. Anyone for a cup of tea?'

Chapter 7

Kids, again

My next placement was on the children's ward. As this was a very general hospital, this was by its nature a very general sort of children's ward. We admitted the most common and basic ailments, from chest infections to appendectomies. Anything slightly off-kilter would be whisked away to one of the children's hospitals in the area.

Here, the sister in charge was another grumpy maiden, who had devoted her life to nursing and looked so happy in her chosen career — not! She was quite civil to her staff, but terrified most of the parents. As for the children in her care, she didn't have much to do with them, saying they were nosey, smelly and inclined to bite. I later found out she was a cat person and hated dogs as well as her patients!

I had already heard about the window battle, for which she was famous. A child with a fever would be on the bed rather than in it, with light cotton pyjamas on and the windows wide open. Parents would come to visit and immediately close the window afraid their child would catch cold. Sister would then march in, glare at the parents and open the window again.

'But she's cold,' they would plead. 'Look, she's shivering.'

'She had a temperature of 40 and was suffering from a rigor. If we don't get her temperature down she will start having convulsions. Do you want that?' Then she would leave the room muttering to herself. She was right of course, but her bedside manner left a lot to be desired.

One of the upsides to working on pediatrics was the sweet tin. All sweets that came onto the ward were put into a large tin. Some were allocated to the children once a day when appropriate, and shared between the staff all the time. There were far too many sweets for the little tots, and if we hadn't done a bit of stock control it would have got silly.

After a consultant's round one day a very junior doctor started rifling through the hoard, only to be put to shame by a four-year-old shouting, 'You stop pinching the nurses' sweets!'

He did just that, and we all went red as visitors glared at us in horror. Not only were we stealing their children's gifts, but we were stealing their sick children's gifts. Quickly the staff found some urgent jobs that needed doing, and disappeared.

There were two children I nursed back then that I will never forget, and the first was Charlie.

Charlie was 18 months old and was being investigated for type 1 diabetes. This meant testing his wee when we could manage to get a sample, which was not easy. Because of this, the most reliable test for his glycemia (sugar) levels was gained by a finger-prick blood test.

Now back in the day this was taken by a technician, and the test was done in the lab. No handy little kit, which meant we couldn't do it. I was glad this job didn't fall on the nurses as Charlie had to have blood taken every four hours. At first he would curl up in his cot and scream. It took four of us to try and calm him and hold him still while the finger prick was administered. Then one of us would scoop him up, cuddle him and take him off to play with the toys. Good nurse, bad nurse.

However, after two weeks of this, one day he amazed us all. As he saw the lab tech come onto the ward in her white coat, he stood at the end of his cot, held out his finger, and started sobbing. We all felt bad, but not as bad as the young lady who had to do the dirty deed.

Needles it was going to be for Charlie, for the rest of his life, so it was good he was starting to get used to them so quickly.

The other patient was not so lucky. Jobe was a 13-year-old orphan who came to us from one of the children's hospitals who could do nothing more for him. He was suffering from acute leukemia and had come to us to die. Harsh, but true.

He had no one, and therefore very few visitors. He was put in a side ward and lay on his bed looking rejected and pathetic. We all felt sorry for him and did our best to cheer him up, which was not easy, but we tried. The one thing that could get him excited was football, and more to the point Liverpool Football Club.

Now it just so happened that Liverpool was in the FA Cup final that year with Arsenal, and it was while we had this young man on the ward. I had the idea we could ask some of the Liverpool players to come and visit him, but when I put this to sister she went very quiet and told me that I was not to pursue this matter because the patient was far too ill, and I also had to think of the other children on the ward.

The staff were all very disappointed by this, but sister's word was law. So that was that.

However, sister was off on the day of the cup final — well, she would be, it was a Saturday after all. We decorated Jobe's room in red and white, bought him a Liverpool shirt and managed somehow to get a TV so he could watch the match.

We also took turns sitting in his room and cheered on his team with him. After all, it's no fun watching these things on your own, is it?

I have never, since 1966, wanted a team to win so much. But in extra time Arsenal scored, beating Liverpool 2-1. Jobe was gutted. I was gutted. We all felt let down.

I cried when I met my boyfriend. 'What's wrong?' he asked, not quite sure why a football match had upset me so much.

When I explained the reason, he just shrugged his shoulders and said, 'It's only a game.'

I then had my days off and when I went back on duty he was very ill indeed. He was bleeding from every orifice and was having a blood transfusion. Why? Well, as medical professionals we felt we should do something — anything — but as one of the doctors said. 'It's a losing battle. We can't get the blood into him quickly enough.'

That night, according to the report, he had a cardiac arrest, and his bed was empty the next day as if he had never been there at all. I thought I would cry, but I didn't. I felt relieved that his pain was over, and then I felt guilty because I didn't cry.

I realised then that being a nurse could be crap at times, and it wasn't the last time I thought that in my career.

Chapter 8

Nights!

We had two weeks in study block next. This was how our classroom training was organised. We completed two rounds of placements of 12 weeks each, and then two weeks devoted to studying, and of course, we all studied each night after an eight-hour shift when we were mentally and physically exhausted. No, I lie, we didn't.

Book work didn't come into the conversation until the next study block loomed before us.

This had its benefits, as it was nine to five, Monday to Friday. But it also meant a lot of reading, lectures and an end of block exam. It was a bit like lock gates on a canal. You had to negotiate one lot before you could reach the next. It wasn't easy, at least not for me, and I suspect for many of my colleagues as well.

We also had an interview with sister tutor about the ward reports from our first two placements. Much to my surprise and relief mine were quite good, and she seemed pleased with me. Maybe I was doing something right after all.

After scraping through my exam, with a must-try-harder mark on the bottom, our set was free for another two weeks' holiday. We waved Mary goodbye — yes, she did come back and now only cried every third night, so she was making progress — and then it was off to our homes.

That was the other thing about training fifty years ago. For the duration of your training your holidays were planned out for you, and you could NEVER change them. It didn't get much better for newly-qualified staff either, as they were at the bottom of the pecking order when holidays were claimed. I knew of one new staff nurse who had to change her wedding plans to fit in with the ward's off-duty.

I never went away when I was off, so it didn't matter to me. I was quite happy being at home and being made a fuss of by mum. I couldn't afford a holiday even if I'd wanted one, so I never minded that some of my friends were jetting off to sun, sea and sex. They had rich parents who paid for their holidays; I didn't.

I did, however, have fun. Trips to the cinema, McDonald's, and Liverpool or Manchester to try and find some bargains with my non-nursing friend (I did only have one) were all I required to make me happy.

Two days before the holiday was over I had to nip into the School of Nursing to find out where I would be working next, and then I could go and get my off duty. When I scanned the list for my name, I saw I was back on women's medical, my first ward. My heart plummeted. This meant only one thing: night duty. I was approaching the end of my first year and I was going to be on nights. My third ward. I was scared stiff.

I didn't get any sleep at all before my first 12-hour nightshift. I wasn't tired, but I was full of anxiety. I got into my uniform and went to have some supper before I went on duty. All the girls looked as down in the mouth as me.

One very pretty nurse who was in the set before ours smiled at me. 'You're on ward 5 tonight with me.' Relief!

'Oh! Hello. I'm Carol.'

'Hi, I'm Maggie and it's my second week of nights on this ward. You're unlucky to get nights during your first year. They usually don't expect you to do them until you're in your second.' She had just passed that milestone.

As we walked across to the hospital from the nurses' home Maggie told me a little of what to expect. 'Most of the work's done when we get there, to be fair. We just have to give the drinks out and settle them down for the night, and after that it's just bedpans and turns.' She made it sound almost better than days.

We had the handover from sister and then got to it. There were thirty patients. Two of these were sick-noted (not expected to live very long), and 'the night sister' was only a phone call away.

The drinks trolley went round and we helped those who couldn't manage on there own, and then started to lie people down, tuck people up and generally try and get the ward quiet.

One very poorly lady was in a side ward. Her breathing was noisy and laboured and she was an awful colour. I went and checked her pulse, and made sure she was getting the right amount of oxygen. The other very sick patient was at the top of the ward by the sister's office, and she was asleep.

We sat in the middle of the ward at the nurses' station with just a desk lamp on. From here we could hear and/or see all the patients, except for the side ward which required regular visits. It was a quiet night, and the occasional bell asking for a bedpan or a drink of water broke up the monotony.

Night sister did her first round at about midnight. 'Now I'm going for my meal break,' she told us pointedly, and left us to it. Lucky her. We had to make do with a sandwich and a cup of tea on the ward, as we didn't have enough staff to cover for meal breaks.

That's when it all kicked off. Someone near the top of the ward called out in pain. I ran up to the cry for help to see what the emergency was — and it was just that, an emergency!

A woman was clutching her chest and screaming that she was going to die. 'I'm having another heart attack,' she shouted as she grabbed my arm very tightly. Maggie was right behind me. 'Phone for night sister and a doctor,' I said, in the calmest voice I could muster.

'What?' Maggie looked more terrified than the patient.

'Night sister and a doctor, now!'

Maggie ran down the ward and called the switchboard. I couldn't hear what she was saying for all the gasping for breath and swearing that was going on, and that was only me. Suddenly the patient vomited, a lot, all over my uniform, and then she collapsed. I felt for a pulse and there was one there, though weak and threadlike.

It seemed like an age, but sister and three doctors turned up all at the same time. The curtains were pulled around the bed and I was told to go and clean myself up. I did feel slightly put out by this, as I had been ready to do CPR and wasn't given the chance.

I found Maggie, white and shaking, still by the phone. 'Is she ... is she dead?'

'Well, she wasn't when I left her,' I said, and shrugged.

In the sluice I took off my apron, which had taken the worst of the vomit, and towelled the rest off as best I could.

When I got back to the ward the night sister was talking to Maggie. I walked quickly towards them, not wanting to miss out on the gory details. 'Has she croaked?' It just came out. I couldn't help myself. Night sister gave me a look that could have frozen cod straight from the trawler. 'No, nurse, she hasn't. She had a bad case of indigestion and a fainting episode. Now get her cleaned up and settled. I'm going to go and finish my now cold meal.' She glared at us both and flounced away.

Meanwhile we sorted out our patient, who was back asleep by the time we got halfway down the ward.

'I'll just check on the side ward,' Maggie said, as I went to dispose of the soiled linen. My posterior had just hit the chair when I heard an earth-shattering scream that had my nerves jangling again. This time it had come from the side ward. I ran in to find Maggie hysterical and one very dead patient in the bed.

'Night sister is going to love this,' I said to myself.

***

After that, nights settled into a normal routine. I didn't see Maggie again. She was replaced by a third-year student who was not pleased about this reshuffle, as she was about to take her final exams. However, she was efficient, took charge and I just tagged along behind. She also spent a great deal of time with her head in a book revising, and left me to do most of the jobs that didn't need two people. This was fine with me, as any little things that might go wrong would be down to her, not me.

As for Maggie, I believe she was asked to reconsider her career choice, and I heard a rumour that she went into accountancy. Hopefully they don't get many dead people in that job.

Chapter 9

Out on my ear

I was just about to go into my second year and had, that week, started on women's orthopaedics when I got called into home sister's office. On the way, I was racking my brain to try and remember what I'd done wrong.

All right, my room was next to the fire escape, and I did let an awful lot of people through it in the early hours of the morning, but that happened all the time, and at other fire escapes as well.

I got a bit fed up with it, especially on Friday, Saturday and Sunday nights. I was in and out of bed more often than a person with a bladder infection. Sorry, is that too much information?

I knocked tentatively on her door. 'Come.' In I went. 'Ah, Nurse. Come and sit down.'

I sat right on the edge of my seat, ready to flee should the need arise. 'Now nurse, you have lived in the home for, let me see...' She peered at a piece of paper over her glasses 'Twelve months. Is that right?'

'Yes, sister.'

'And have you been happy here?'

'Yes, sister.'

I relaxed a little

'Good.'

'Yes, sister.'

'But am I right in thinking you don't live very far away?' She consulted a list in her hand.

'Yes, sister.'

'Good.'

'Is it?'

'Nurse, we have a new intake soon, and half of this set are from Hong Kong.'

'Oh.'

'And we are short of accommodation.'

'Are we?'

'Yes, nurse. So, I presume you can guess what I'm about to ask you?' A smile.

'No, sister.'

At this she sighed. 'Would you be prepared to live out from next week?'

'What?'

'We are asking all the local student nurses to move out, so that these new nurses can have a room.'

'But it will be a problem with the bus times and my shifts,' I pleaded.

'I'm sure you will find a way, nurse.' The smile this time was more of a grimace.

'I don't live that close, not really.'

'But you do live closer than Hong Kong.'

That I couldn't argue with. And the conversation, such as it was, came to an end.

So, it came to pass that one week later I packed my lovely little room into a taxi, left my friends, moved out of the nurses' home, and headed home. I didn't have an issue with living at home apart from, as I had pointed out, public transport.

The buses wouldn't get me to work in time for an early shift, and they were few and far between after six in the evening, so after a late shift it would take hours to get home. We didn't have a car, and I couldn't drive, or afford lessons, let alone a vehicle if I managed to pass my test. It was a conundrum.

As a cadet we did nine to five so this was never an issue, and I hoped that Pam, who also lived in my town, might be able to offer a lift on occasion. 'I said no,' she told me calmly. 'I'm not trudging in each day with the shifts we have to do.'

'You could say no?'

'Of course you could. You are such a pushover.' Strangely, that made me feel as if I'd been picked on.

I had a word with my new ward sister and asked for as many late starts as she could manage to give me. She was very obliging, and I had all late shifts on my first week of living at home, but I had to leave home at ten in the morning and was getting home between ten and eleven at night. Not good.

It was clear that this wasn't going to work, and I went to sister tutor to ask her advice. Her reply was, 'I'm sorry, Nurse, but my hands are tied when it comes to the nurses' accommodation.'

I managed to get in twenty minutes late on each early, and I was pushing my luck as far as the sister was concerned. She had me in the office on more than one occasion and told me to sort something out.

I was at a loss to what the solution might be when fate interceded and made my mind up for me.

It came out of the blue. No one saw how ill she was. I was too busy getting to work and back, and my dad just accepted her 'don't fuss, it's nothing,' plea.

Mum collapsed. She was very poorly with pneumonia. Dad couldn't cope, and I had no choice. I took a sabbatical from my training — that is, resigned — and signed on for unemployment benefit, also known as 'the dole.'

And that was the end of part one of my nursing career. At the time I fully intended to go back when Mum was better, but that just didn't happen.

PART TWO
1980-1985

Chapter 10

Am I a Time Lord?

'I want to go back to nursing.'

'What?' My husband looked at me as if I had just told him I'd made a pact with the devil for our beautiful children's souls in return for a Bakewell tart. 'Are you mad?'

'Probably.'

'What about childcare?'

'I've thought about that.'

'Good. Because I don't think a four-year-old and a two-year-old could manage on their own.'

I had thought about little else since this idea had started to percolate in my mind. It mainly revolved around my dad, who spent a lot of time with us anyway and would happily help.

'I'd apply now for next September when the baby is due to start nursery and Dan starts school.'

I think my husband was relived I wasn't about to try and make this fantasy a reality straightaway.

Over the next few months we discussed all the pro and cons, and there seemed to be more cons than pros, to be honest. However, him indoors was very supportive and the next thing I knew I was heading for the School of Nursing at the local hospital, close to where I now lived, for an interview.

A man and a deputy matron sat behind a desk and inter-rogated (sorry) interviewed me, asking me why I had left my training last time, why I wanted to return, and how on earth I was going to cope with my domestic arrangements, work shifts and study.

'For example,' said the man, who introduced himself as the director of nursing, 'what would you do if one of your children were sick?'

'It depends on how sick they were. If they had a cold or tummy upset, well, my husband can just as easily take time off work as I can. But if they were really poorly, I'd be with them, of course.' 'Would you, now?' The man clasped his hands together and learned forward.

'Yes. And any good mother who says differently would be lying to you.' That's it, I thought, just blown it.

'A very honest answer, if I might say so.' This came from the deputy matron, who smiled at me.

'And what happens if you get pregnant again during your training?' The man looked at me with scorn.

'I don't think you can ask that,' said the deputy matron.

'I think I just did.' He wasn't impressed that she dared to challenge his line of questioning. 'It takes a lot of time and money to train these nurses.' He was now talking to her, not me. 'I think we have the right to know if they might leave in the middle of it all.'

'But you can't ask personal questions like that.' I felt as if I was intruding on this little domestic and cleared my throat.

The man took a breath and turned his attention to me again. 'Well, we will consider you for the 2-year course to become an enrolled nurse. You couldn't possibly manage the 3-year course for registration.'

'Why not?' asked the deputy matron. 'She has the right exam results to do that.'

This time he ignored her completely. 'You will hear our decision by post within the next week. Thank you for attending today.'

With that I was dismissed, and I closed the door on what was now becoming a heated debate in the interview room.

Outside sat three other women waiting to go in, listening to the raised voices and looking very uncomfortable. 'Good luck,' I said, and left them to it.

***

September 1980 came around far too quickly, and in the months leading up to that date I had changed my mind so many times that him indoors refused to talk about it anymore. 'Look, go, give it a chance, and if it doesn't work out — well, you tried, didn't you?'

'Yes, but...'

'Yes but, no but. This is my last word on the subject.' And it was.

Dad was installed in the spare bedroom, and took both children to school, and picked them up at four o'clock. All I had to do was go and learn how to be a nurse, again.

The eight-week introduction course saw a group of twenty starting their nursing career. The youngest in the group was only 17 but would be 18 in eighteen in two weeks, and the oldest was 45 and had decided she wanted a career now that her children were off her hands.

Once again, we all gelled well as a set of women who wanted the same thing (there were no men this time). We all wanted to do two years' training and become state enrolled nurses at the end of it. Simple as.

I found the theory much easier this time around, and of course the practical stuff at that level I could do in my sleep. This gave me new-found confidence and I enjoyed those first eight weeks in the training school.

The end of block exam was multiple choice. No long answers to write, no essays. All we had to do is tick a box. We had three to choose from, and therefore a one-in-three chance of getting it right.

There were fifty questions and I presumed this was a tried and tested way of finding out what knowledge had sunk in during that first eight weeks.

I hate to brag, but I found the exam easy and got 95%. I'm not sure what happened to the other 5%, but as the pass mark was 65%, I was well clear. We all passed with decent marks and were keen to go onto our first wards the following week and get stuck in.

I hadn't told anyone that I'd started nursing originally at 17, as I thought people might expect more from me. I told anyone that might be interested it was just life's experiences that had helped me do so well on the introduction course.

Chapter 11

Here we go again

My first ward was a mixed medical ward. I was on there with another pupil from my group and I must admit I felt at home straight away. The staff were nice, the patients were ill, so all in all a truly good learning environment for all the nervous first years.

The ward had four 6-bedded bays, two for the males and two for the females. It also had four cubicles and a side ward.

We were divided into teams and each nurse was given up to six patients who were her responsibility during that shift. As we were very new pupils (learners training be an enrolled nurses were called pupil nurses, and those training to be SRN were called students,) we got just 3 patients each to care for: one ready for home, so not needing much attention at all; one on the road to recovery so requiring a bit more TLC; and one poorly one who would take up most of your time.

The work was interesting and not too demanding mentally, but I got so tired that I was usually asleep by nine each night and found it very difficult to get out of bed in the morning. Unlike my younger colleagues, I had to get up at 7 am come what may, even on a late shift or day off, as I had two demanding children to get sorted and if I was on a late, I would often prepare a meal and do some housework before I went off to work.

The upside was that I found the job stimulating and of course the extra money came in very handy — yes, we actually got a salary back in the day.

As I usually got my two days off between Monday and Friday, and at least one late shift in those five days, meaning the domestic side of life wasn't as bad as I had thought. Him indoors took charge at the weekends, and I got to take the children to school/nursery 3 times a week.

I was halfway through my first eight-week placement when I had a very bad day. After having my patients allocated to me, I had started with all the routine stuff when I was called to a side ward to one of 'my' patients.

'What's up, Rob?' I asked as I breezed into his room and cancelled the call bell. But I could see straight away he wasn't well. Now you might say if he was well, he shouldn't be in a hospital.

And he wouldn't be by 2 pm today. He was my 'ready for discharge patient.' After suffering a major heart attack at the age of 48 he was now well on the road to recovery, or so we thought.

Randy Rob, as he was affectionally known, had a very complicated sex life. Married with children, he also had 2 mistresses on the go, and they all visited him.

Logistically, it was a nightmare being on the look-out for one woman coming in and getting rid of the woman who was in his room through the French doors. The most important thing was to make sure both his fancy women were well and truly out of the building before Randy Rob's wife turned up. The medical consultant suggested that this lifestyle might have contributed to his ill health (really, do you think?).

When I went into his room Rob was sitting up clutching his chest and his face was grey. 'Pain,' was about all he could manage, and then he collapsed. Adrenaline took over. I hit the emergency buzzer and pulled Rob flat on the bed, then felt for a pulse, and checked his breathing. Nothing. The cheating bastard had arrested. I jumped on top of him and started chest compression just as the ward's staff nurse came in. 'Am I interrupting something?' she joked. But then she saw the look on my face and gathered that I wasn't having a quickie with Randy Rob, I was trying to save his life.

Soon the team were working on him. We all tried our best, but unlike most hospital dramas, people who suffered cardiac arrests usually died, and Randy Rob was one of those statistics.

We hate losing a patient, especially when they are young and getting better. It's taken as a personal insult, and then blame sets in. What didn't we see? Was he on the right meds? Was he taking the meds that we gave him? But sometimes you must just accept that it didn't matter what you did, or didn't do, nothing was going to save that patient.

Sister came on duty as we were clearing up the mess, and believe me there was some mess to be cleared up. She was quickly put in the picture and she asked if his wife had been informed.

I shrugged, and so did the nurse with me. We had been somewhat too busy to think about such matters.

Sister did that job we all dreaded, phoning a relative to say that their loved one had died, though we avoided the D-word as much as possible. They have passed away, passed over, slipped away, never regained consciousness, we did everything we could but....

I remember one lady who had sat with her dying mother for days. At last the staff had persuaded her to go home and have a rest. She would only agree to this if we promised to call her with any change at all, and she would come straight back in.

Unfortunately, her mother was found dead by the night staff at around six the next morning. The nurse in charge didn't call her daughter until seven. 'I'm afraid your mum's condition has got a lot worse,' she lied.

The daughter arrived within twenty minutes. 'How is she?' she asked, panting.

The staff nurse took her into the office. 'I'm so sorry, but she passed away a few minutes ago. She went very quickly.'

The woman nodded and started to cry. 'She wasn't alone, was she, when she passed?'

'Of course not,' reassured the nurse.

I asked her about this later. 'Well she wasn't alone. She was with five other patients in the bay,' she said as she lit up a fag and shrugged. It's all about perception.

My bad day ended when my very sick patient who was 88 also arrested. He was still very poorly, and in a side ward attached to many monitors and machines, which buzzed loudly when the heart stopped beating rhythmically. Call it early warning, but we managed to revive him, and when I went off duty feeling depleted and upset, it was still touch and go if he would make it through the night. Him indoors didn't help. 'They'll be calling you Nurse Death at this rate,', he joked. I didn't laugh.

I had two days off after this, and when I went back in was very surprised to see the 88-year-old sitting up in bed reading The Times. 'Hello,' I said with a big smile on my face, thinking miracles do happen. 'How are you?'

He folded his paper slowly, took off his glasses and then spoke. 'How am I? I'll tell you how I am. I'm bloody furious, that's how I am!'

'What?'

'Why on earth didn't you leave well alone? I should be with my Maker now.'

'But you could have died!'

'Well, girly, I've got news for you; we all have to die sometime. Bloody medical advances.'

That wasn't what I was expecting. There's just no pleasing some people.

Chapter 12

An open and shut case

Men's surgical was my next port of call. I must admit to a great deal of apprehension here. For one thing, I had somehow during my time nursing managed to miss all surgical wards. That's not counting the children's ward at my last hospital which did a few minor ops, and I was never about when these took place, so as I said, that doesn't count.

I had also heard on the grapevine that the senior sister of this ward was a bit of a dragon. 'If she doesn't like the look of you, she makes your life a misery,' I was told during one lunch break.

Well, I didn't want to go down that road again.

On my first morning, after the report, she picked me to team up with. I tried to make myself as inconspicuous as possible in the office, but it hadn't worked. She chatted, I nodded, she told me to do things, and I did them.

When I went for my break with two other nurses, they teased me, 'who's sisters' blue-eyed nurse then?' I just changed the subject and was relieved she wasn't as bad as I was expecting. Maybe she was nice deep down, and just had a bad reputation?

But no. When we got back to the ward, sister was yelling at a very junior doctor telling him in no uncertain terms that he was a blood-sucking vampire with no empathy for his patients.

Doctor TT, as he was generally known, was from Greece. He was small and spoke with a squeaky voice and no one could pronounce his real name hence the nick name. He had, he told us, worked in the USA where nurses did many of the jobs expected of him in the UK. One such job was to take blood from patients.

Back then nurses never took blood, it wasn't our job. Doctor TT found this very annoying, mainly because he couldn't do it. He was hopeless. So many patients ended up with sore bruised arms, and not a drop of blood in a bottle to go to the lab. There was one time when he went straight through a small artery and that patient did bleed, a lot. All over the bed, and the floor, but still not even a tiny bit managed to gravitate into the bottle.

We dreaded him appearing on the ward to do anything to any of our patients, and often found a much more senior doctor doing his job. I was mystified at first, but then I found out that this dishy doctor was also our sister's boyfriend and would do anything for her.

He told us that Doctor TT didn't want to look after physically sick people, but wanted to be a psychiatrist. I was slightly relieved that this was going to be his job, and at least he wouldn't have to stick needles into people very often. I hoped I would never have to see him in his chosen field. 'Why did his nickname end up as Doctor TT?' I asked. 'His surname begins with D, doesn't it?'

The nice doctor laughed. 'It's not short for his real name, it's short for twisted testicles.'

'What?' I tried not to giggle, but I couldn't help it. So that's why he spoke in such a peculiar way? Probably not, but medical staff can be incredibly cruel to their colleagues given half a chance.

Because our patient turnover was rapid and mostly planned, we were allocated patients on arrival at the ward, who we then admitted and cared for until their discharge. Their stay was longer than today by a country mile, but much quicker than on the medical and orthopaedic wards.

We seldom received emergencies, as such urgent surgical cases usually went straight to theatre from A&E and often then into ICU (Intensive Care Unit) for a while before transferring to this ward.

Mr Good was admitted about three weeks into my surgical placement and I was going to be the nurse that looked after him during my time on duty. He was a tall elderly man, well dressed in expensive clothes, and when I call him a gentleman, I mean that. He was polite, courteous towards women and very quietly spoken. He was brought in for investigations into abdominal pain and weight loss.

'Put him in the first side ward', sister instructed me. It was unusual for this to happen as we reserved that room for very sick patients as a rule, but I suppose we must have been quiet, which was usually the calm before the storm. As I did his observations I chatted away, and he answered when necessary and smiled at me when I told him all was normal.

He was listed the next day for colonoscopy and had an enema that night. This test proved inconclusive, as had all the others he had through his GP and consultant as an outpatient. Usually the next stage would have been a laparotomy, (a surgical incision into the abdominal cavity, for diagnosis in this case,) but medicine now had the technology in the form of a brand-new piece of equipment called an MRI scanner to hopefully make the surgical investigation unnecessary.

We had one in the North West and Mr Good was going to be among the first in the area to benefit from this science. And I was going to escort him there and back, which I was most excited about, and the envy of all my colleagues.

We had a long but interesting day. The ambulance dropped us off at the door of a very large city hospital and then we had to circumnavigate miles of corridors to find the radiography department, just to be told we were in the wrong place. 'The scanner,' I was informed in a most reverent voice that had me almost genuflecting, 'is housed in its own department.' We were pointed in the right direction and eventually located it. I was fascinated by all the bells and whistles, and a very nice man explained to me how it all worked. He was wasting his time, bless him, I didn't understand a word he said, but he was so enthusiastic I just smiled in all the right places.

After it was all done and dusted, we went into a small café and waited for our transport. Mr Good insisted I sat down and then went and bought me a cup of tea and a cake. 'Thanks,' I said, very touched by his kindness, 'but I think you'll find I'm supposed to be looking after you.'

'I'm fine,' he said, 'a lot of fuss about nothing. I'm only here because my old boss insisted.' He started asking me why I wanted to be a nurse and before I knew it, I had told him my life story.

'And what did you do for a living?' I asked, still not knowing very much about this man. 'No, let me guess. Solicitor?' He shook his head. 'Accountant?'

'No.'

'Teacher?' Still not right. 'Okay, I give in.'

'Nothing of note. Just a civil servant. Very boring, actually.'

'Really? I was in the civil service before I had my children. Department of Employment.'

'And how long did you do that for?' I didn't even realising it, but he had turned the spotlight back on to me.

Two days later Mr Good went to theatre, as the MRI had shown multiple tumours throughout his body, the largest sitting in his abdomen. When he came back to his room I looked after him as if he were a loved one, as strangely he never seemed to get visitors.

His surgeon was talking to the sister when I went into the office to ask something. 'I've never seen anything like it. Loads of tumours all over the place. Can't imagine what caused them. If he had worked with some sort of toxic substance it might make more sense. All we could do was close again — he won't have long.'

I froze in my tracks. I couldn't believe what I was hearing. Mr Good didn't look that ill. They must be talking about somebody else. But in the report the next day it was made clear just what his prognosis was; death!

'We will get him as well as possible, and then he can go home. That's what he wants, apparently,' the sister informed us. 'The physio will be round later to do some breathing exercises with him.'

I didn't know what to say to Mr Good when I went into his room. I was relieved that he was still very sleepy, and he just smiled and said, 'Ah, here is my favourite nurse,' which just made me want to cry.

After lunch I saw the physio in his room. She had him sat up leaning against the bed table with a pillow supporting his abdomen, getting him to cough. I was just going to go into the sluice when she came hurrying to get me. 'Nurse,' she said urgently, 'can you come, please. This doesn't look right to me.'

I followed her. Mr Good was leaning back against a sea of pillows, and his guts were lying on the outside of his body. 'That's not right, is it?' said the physio.

I ran out of the side ward into the treatment room, grabbed some sterile gauze and saline, and shouted for help, without trying to sound as panicked as I was feeling.

Soon the doctor was there. He called the consultant, who called the anaesthetist, and they took Mr Good back to theatre. I was congratulated for my quick thinking, which didn't sink in. I was more horrified by what I'd seen than I was prepared to admit.

Mr Good died that night in ICU. I wish I'd known more about him, but I did hear that he had worked for MI6. Was that true? I'll never know, but I'd like to believe it.

Chapter 13

Nasty nurses

Men's surgical was followed by a week in study block and then 2 weeks' annual leave, which I was in urgent need of. I was exhausted both physically and mentally by now, and needed this stretch to catch up on domestic chores, seeing friends and family, and having some extra sleep.

But sod's law happens. Five days into my leave I came down with a very nasty virus which saw me in bed for three days, so him indoors not only had all his usual duties to do, but he also had me to look after. When I started back at work I wasn't completely recovered, and I think this was a contributory factor in what followed.

My next placement was a geriatric ward — a term which is still used in some places, and I always thought it to be a horrible word. It was classed as an assessment ward. Patients would either get well and go home, die, or be transferred to one of the three long-stay wards on the perimeter of the hospital. There were very few nursing homes in those days, but then people didn't live as long as they do now, so it all balanced out in the end.

For me this was just an extension of a medical ward, except the patients were older. We saw mostly stroke patients, or as they were labelled then, CVA patients (Cerebrovascular Accident).

We also saw a lot of patients with chest infections and urinary tract infections. This, then, was going to be my bread and butter for the next eight weeks.

I wasn't fazed by the prospect of this ward until I met two bitches from hell in the form of the two enrolled nurses who ran the ward while the nice but ineffectual sister sat in the office. At this point I should emphasize that they were horrible to all trainee nurses, not just me. To begin with I let it go over my head, and the students would bitch about the nurses as much as they did about us, which sort of balanced things out.

Then I had a practically stressful day. I hadn't slept for two nights as my little girl was ill with m virus, I still didn't feel very well myself, and that was the day they had a real go at me. I couldn't do a thing right. I was called stupid and incompetent, and the final straw was when I came back from my break.

'Enjoy your tea and toast, did you?' asked one of the bitches.

'Yes, thanks.'

'So glad. But while you were doing that, we had to get Mrs Brown's drip re-sited because her saline ran through and had to clean up where Mrs Smith's catheter bag flooded the floor. And if I'm not mistaken they are both your patients!' She wasn't just telling me off she was shouting at me in the middle of the ward, arms crossed and glaring.

'I'm sorry, but I asked someone to keep an eye on them for me.'

'They are YOUR responsibility, not someone else's. Now go and tidy the linen cupboard. At least you can't do any harm in there.' I almost ran to this hiding place, shut the door behind me, and began to cry.

I cried, and I cried. I couldn't stop crying. After some time, I have no idea how long, a third-year student nurse came in looking for something. She did a double-take when she saw the state of me, but she didn't need to ask why, because she had been on the ward when the bitch had fired both barrels at me.

'Oh, don't let that cow do this to you,' she said as she sat next to me, and put her arm around my shoulder. This just made me worse and the uncontrollable sobbing started again.

'I'm going to the School of Nursing. It's ridiculous. They can't treat people like this.'

Just then the bitch popped her head around the door to see where all her staff were disappearing to. 'Whatever is the matter?' she asked, with real concern in her voice.

'As if you don't know.' The third-year stood and faced her. 'You! That's what the matter is. I'm reporting you to the school. Let's see how you get on when they remove all the learners from this ward. You will have to actually do some work.' With that she made a very good exit, leaving the accused standing with her mouth opening and closing like a fish.

The enrolled nurse then came and sat next to me. 'I'm so sorry. It's nothing personal. We just try and toughen learners up here.'

'I'm working in a hospital,' I managed, 'not the army.'

I was treated like I was made of china after this incident, and the bitches started being nice to all the other students and pupils on the ward. We suspect that they had been visited by someone from the School of Nursing and told off, but we never got to find out. I wondered just how long they could be nice before the bitches came back?

Chapter 14

Another Casualty

It couldn't have been a more different experience than my first one on casualty, now called A&E.

The staff were jolly, keen to teach, and grateful for the help that we trainee nurses could give to them.

The two-year course was one of 'here instead of there, this department instead of that department.' We either did A&E or theatre, orthopaedics or gynae. The Gods that selected which of us did what must have been looking down on me, as I got the better deals — in my opinion, at any rate.

Every day on A&E was different and unpredictable, which is why it was so exciting and a good training placement. Also, there were several dishy doctors for the unattached to drool over. One SHO (senior house officer) was tall, dark and handsome with a southern Irish lilt to his voice that sounded like melted dark chocolate pouring onto skin. Oops sorry, flipped out there. But everyone was in love with him a bit, and he didn't seem to know what effect he had on the opposite sex, so I can only presume he was gay.

But he was also a very kind person and brilliant with the patients, both male and female. He had the nickname of the Irish Idol, but sadly his rotation was ending just as ours started, and then he went off to another hospital and left many a broken heart behind. But enough of this Mills and Boon nonsense; back to reality.

Our senior sister was not one to be messed with. She was fair to all, would come down on you like a ton of bricks if you did something wrong after being shown the right way to do it, and it didn't matter if you were the cleaner or a consultant, everyone was treated the same way. She also gave the best parties as well, and I went to two in the short time that I was on A&E, plus all the 'let's go for a drink after work' suggestions. It must be because these medics are dealing with horrible things every day that they need to take life by the throat and strangle every last bit of joy out of it. Either that or they drink to blot out the terrible bits. To be honest, I think it was a bit of both.

I can remember the standoff sister had with a patient once who had dialed 999 because she had something in her eye. This woman lived about as far away as it was possible and still be brought to our A&E. The ambulance crew were not amused, but kept a professional front as they handed her over to us.

The problem turned out to be grit, which the doctor washed out. He put some antibiotic cream in her eye, covered it with a patch and told her to see her GP if she had further problems with it. Everyone bit their tongue until she requested an ambulance to take her home.

The receptionist laughed out loud. 'We are not a taxi service, madame. But I can call you one.'

The patient stood her ground, demanding to speak to the person in charge. 'Sister,' yelled the receptionist, 'this lady wants an ambulance to take her home.' The whole department heard this, plus other waiting patients.

Sister took this lady into her office. We could all hear what sister was shouting, and it went something like this. 'Time wasting fool! How would you feel if your mother was dying and the ambulance couldn't get there because some IDIOT had called 999 for something so trivial? You've no consideration. And NO, you can't have an ambulance to take you home.'

The accused intervened when she could, but as she was speaking in a normal voice, we didn't get to hear that side of the conversation. Eventually, she came out with 'I'm going to report you for this,' thrown over her shoulder as she left the room. Then she walked into a wall and knocked herself out.

The patient ended up being in overnight for observations. Her brother picked her up the next day, and as far as we know she didn't complain, but then karma does have a way of working things out all on its own.

A lot happened in the eight weeks I was on this department, so I'm going to divide my experiences into the saddest, the most tragic and the funniest things that I can remember.

The saddest:

'They have just brought a cot death in. Do you want to see the body?' Quite a brutal start to a shift, don't you think?

I wasn't sure what to say. My first reaction was 'No way', but as the nurse who had asked me pointed out, better now than having to face it further down the line as an emergency, and maybe having no choice but to deal with it.

I considered it for a while as I went around and did the morning checks on the equipment. It was almost a religious experience going and checking oxygen, suction, deliberators, resus drugs — all things that on other wards didn't get done as often as they should, as I was to find out later in my training, quite a few times.

By the time I had finished this routine task I had made my mind up that I did want — no that's not the right word, I definitely didn't WANT to see a dead baby, not now, not ever. No, I needed to see this tiny soul in the hope that one day I might be able to help some distraught family in similar circumstances instead of falling to pieces in front of them. Not helpful.

I steeled myself as I went into the screened-off cubicle with the other nurse. I don't know what I was expecting, but all I could see was a doll, lying lifeless, perfect in every way. I say doll because my brain wouldn't let me think of this as anything else.

'What happened?' I asked in a quiet voice.

'They don't know. They found their baby like this at six this morning and called for an ambulance. But it was too late.'

'Where are they? The parents, I mean.'

'At the police station, giving statements.'

'Why?'

She just shrugged. 'Procedure. This little one is waiting to go to for a post-mortem.'

'What!' I was horrified.

'And the police will be taking things from the house for forensic examination.'

'They don't think the parents...?' I left the question hanging.

'Probably not. But as I said, it's procedure.'

I went home that evening and told him indoors all about it, minus names. I often did this but never brought the real person into the discussion. We didn't get counselling then for traumatic events, and he is a very good listener.

'Just think.' I rabbited on, 'you just found your child dead, then the police take you away to make a statement, raid your home for evidence and you have the horror of your tiny baby being cut up.' Even I winced when I said that.

'Well, they are just doing their job, love.'

'But why? Don't you think they have been through enough?'

'Why? In case it wasn't a natural death, I suppose.'

'It's horrible. I don't think it's necessary.'

'I do.'

This answer shocked me. 'What? But who are they helping?'

'The next baby that might die by unnatural causes, but survives because of previous investigations, and the parents of those that have died a natural death. Want another cup of tea?'

Funny:

He was in full biker's garb as he ran into the reception. Round hat, huge goggles and gauntlets

protecting his hands. 'Has a young girl of fourteen been admitted?' he gasped as he leaned against the desk trying to get his breath back.

'Name?' asked the receptionist.

'Fred Brown.'

'Not yours. The girl'.'

'What? Oh yes. Sally Brown. She's about this tall.' He held up his hand to indicate her height. 'And she has long blond hair. Oh, please don't say she is badly hurt!'

'No. She's not here. What happened?'

'I picked her up from school, and when I got home, she wasn't on the back of the bike.'

We all tried very hard not to laugh; after all this poor lass might be seriously hurt in a ditch somewhere at the side of the road.

'I suggest you go home and if there is no sign of her, call the police. Give me your phone number and if she turns up here, we will let you know.'

'Yes. Yes, of course. Thank you.' He scribbled down a number and then he left as quickly as he had arrived.

The day moved on and it wasn't until almost 5 pm that one of the nurses brought up the subject of the missing girl. 'I'll call and see if she turned up,' said the receptionist. As she punched in the number we stood around, too nosey to go off shift without a resolution to this mystery.

After a short conversation, the receptionist said, 'Well, I'm glad she is okay. That's all right, Mr Brown.' She put the phone down and started laughing.

'Well?' I asked for the collective group.

'Apparently his daughter's skirt was caught in the seat. She stood up at the first set of traffic lights to fix it, and her dad went off without her when the lights changed.' We all laughed but more in relief than anything.

'How did she get home?' someone asked.

'Her friend was in the car with her mum behind, and they took her home. All's well that ends well!'

For a change, what could have been a tragic incident turned out to have a simple and harmless explanation. However, I did wonder how long it would be before Sally forgave her father. Thank goodness there was nothing like social media back then.

Tragic:

I was on a late shift when twin sisters aged fifteen were brought into the department on blue lights. One was fine, if in shock. The other was an asthmatic in the throes of a respiratory arrest.

Both excellent athletes, they had been taking part in a cross country run for the county. The asthmatic always used her inhaler before events, and carried it with her during races.

Running had made her illness improve over the years, and it's surprising how many athletes suffer from asthma which we never know about.

She had collapsed halfway round the course. Being unconscious, she was unable to use her inhaler, and by the time the paramedics got to her she was in a very critical state. They managed to stabilize her and were on their way in when she stopped breathing.

I was very much part of the team that dealt with this emergency. I stood with the anaesthetist as he put a tube down her throat so that a machine could breathe for her, and I used suction to help clear the mouth and throat of secretions.

We had just attached her to a respirator and were about to move her to ICU when the curtains flew open and one of our nurses stood there, pale and shaking. The patient was her daughter.

We all felt for this poor woman, and as she accompanied her child to the unit. I looked at the anaesthetist I'd been working so closely with — a man I'd never seen before, and whom I never saw again. He just shook his head slowly. He didn't need to say anything Even I, with my limited medical experience, knew the outcome of this wasn't going to be a positive one.

I went home that night and sat alone in the dark. It was very unusual for this to happen, but him indoors had gone out, the children were asleep in bed, and the babysitter had her coat on and was heading for the door even before I had taken mine off.

I needed to be alone, and as I drank a whiskey by the light of the fire, I took refuge in the fact that we had done everything, and I mean everything, to revive that poor girl. But sometimes you're on a hiding to nothing.

Chapter 15

Don't follow me, I'm lost!

I couldn't quite believe it, but I was just about to enter my second year as a pupil nurse. The time had flown by, and I had fought through exhaustion, pain and 'Why am I doing this to myself?' so many times to get here.

I hurt my back lifting a patient — a manoeuvre we wouldn't even attempt these days, but then it was just sheer strength in numbers that got people moved. My GP said I needed two months to recover, but the School of Nursing said two weeks, so two weeks it was. They fitted me with a corset that made me look ridiculous and didn't seem to do much in the way of helping my back, and many years later I needed surgery on my spine. Maybe I should have listened to my GP all that time ago...

Being a second-year put the fear of God into me. One day you weren't expected to know anything, and the next day everyone thought you were a font of all knowledge. First-year student nurses, even doctors, would look to you for guidance.

The other scary aspect of this rise to power was that my finals would soon be hurtling towards me.

In my first year, finals were so far away it didn't even enter my head that they would ever actually happen, and now our intake all knew that they were just around the corner.

My next placement was nights on the medical ward that I had been on for my first eight weeks after the introduction training. I was to do seven nights on and seven off.

These nights started at 8 pm and finished at 8 am. I wasn't worried about the actual night duty because there were enough staff to manage. We had an enrolled nurse in charge of our ward and a charge nurse (male sister) in charge of the unit. Charlie was one of the finest nurses I have ever worked with. He got the best out of his staff and all the patients thought he was the bee's knees.

Apart from fighting tiredness, nights were all right. By the third night I felt like a zombie, by the seventh I was fine. Then on the first two nights I was off I couldn't sleep, and it took me the whole seven days off to regulate myself to being up during the day and sleeping at night. I'd just cracked that when I was back on nights and it all started again.

My time on this ward was quite uneventful, and I often felt as if we were just babysitting. Especially when it came to Emily.

Emily had dementia and was in the hospital because she had been suffering from a urinary tract infection. This had made the poor woman more confused than normal. She would sleep all day and then haunt the night staff. The day staff thought this was great, and to be fair we didn't mind. We had the time to occupy her, and she would often come and sit outside the sister's office with us as this was where we would set up for the night. It was the optimal position for being able to hear noises from both corridors, but far away enough not to disturb the patients as we talked quietly to each other.

Once Emily had 'helped' us do the night drinks and settle the patients down we would often play board games to help keep us alert. She would sit with us and move our counters without

hesitation and we then couldn't remember where we were. It made the contest interesting and funny, so we just went along with it.

We made the mistake one night of not answering a bell straight away, as we were so engrossed in Trivial Pursuit. Suddenly a terrifying scream came from one of the women's bays. Three of us rushed in to find Emily trying to get into bed with a very frightened lady who just wanted a painkiller.

That sorted, we went back to our game. Emily wasn't interested in playing with us that night and as we all concentrated on the questions, she raised a bony finger. 'Look,' she said, in a voice that any good psychic would have been proud of. She was pointing to the window behind us.

We all turned around but there was nothing there except the trees blowing outside. 'It's okay Emily,' said the EN, 'it's just the trees.'

'No,' she said again in her best vampire voice, 'the kettle is there.'

We all turned again. Nothing. 'Maybe she wants a drink,' I suggested. 'Would you like a cup of tea, Emily?'

'You can't. The kettle is there.' This time we heard a tap on the window, and all of us jumped up.

'What was that?' said one nurse, clasping her hands together.

'The kettle can fly,' said Emily.

'Come on, Emily. Maybe you should try and get some sleep.'

Tap, tap at the window. Then, before our eyes, a kettle floated down and hung motionless for a few seconds before disappearing again. One girl screamed, and I must admit my heart was thumping in my chest at this point.

'Charlie!' said the EN, and disappeared outside.

A few minutes later she reappeared with Charlie, a kettle which had a suture thread tied to it. His face was a picture. He might have been the nurse in charge, but he did love his practical jokes. 'This one was on the roof trying to scare us with that!' The roof, I should point out, was flat, and it was a single-storey building.

'Why?' I asked.

'Just to keep you all on your toes,' said Charlie with a smile, and then he went back to his office.

'He's always up to something,' said the EN, grinning.

Emily had been a witness to all this, and after Charlie had left, she sat down again.

'Are you okay?' I asked, worried that the whole scenario might have upset her.

Emily seemed calm and even serene, which was more than could be said for the staff at that moment. 'Yes,' she said and smiled. I'd never seen her smile before. She had a lovely face when she looked happy.

'That's good.'

'Nurse.'

'Yes, Emily?'

'I told you I'd seen a flying kettle.'

'Yes, you did Emily.'

'See, I'm not stupid,' she said and winked at me.

Chapter 16

I'll make no bones about it

Male orthopaedics. Yes!

You may wonder why I was so pleased with the prospect of my next placement. Firstly, it wasn't the gynae ward, and secondly, it wasn't female orthopaedics.

What is the difference? Broken bones are, after all, broken bones. Well, the difference is this:

Male orthopaedics: *young men who had come off fast bikes and hurt something, rugby players who had torn something, football players who had over stretched something.*

Female orthopaedics: *old ladies with fractured hips.*

I rest my case.

We had men in traction for various reasons such as fractured femurs and back pain, and they were trapped in bed. What they were not was ill. This gave way to lots of jokes, general hilarity and plenty of bed baths.

I would often take on the job of foot care for these patients, as strangely it was one of those things that some nurses hated. When you think of all the other parts of the anatomy we had to touch, both inside and out, feet to me seemed the better body part to be working on. I would cut nails, massage cream into dry skin and then draw funny faces on the bottom of patients' big toes. Yes, I was that person. It made the men on the opposite side of the ward smile, and there was also much laughter when visiting time came around.

This little trick did get me in trouble once, as the owner of the foot I had drawn on tried to see what artwork I had left him with. In doing this his traction fell off and he was in a lot of pain.

Traction was the most common form of treatment for such things as back pain and leg fractures, and involved weights and pulleys. A degree in mechanical engineering might have been more use on orthopaedics than a nursing qualification. Even though we have advanced a great deal in forms of treatment over the years, traction is still used sometimes even now.

Considering myself chastised, I put my creative side on hold and did more of the nursing I was expected to do. I enjoyed this ward more than any I had worked on to date. Not just the light- hearted men we were looking after, who appreciated everything we did for them, but also the mixture of disciplines on this unit. We had the surgical experience, balanced with good nursing care, and all the student and pupil nurses had the chance to expand their knowledge.

While there I was asked if I wanted to go and observe an operation, and I jumped at the chance. I had never been near an operating theatre in my life and thought how interesting it might be.

I was to go to theatre with a man who was having a total hip replacement. I got him ready for his surgery and I'm not sure which of us was the most nervous. But I suppose that was me, since after all, he would be asleep. Would I show myself up, I wondered? Would I pass out? Would there be lots of blood? Might I vomit?

As we went towards the theatre suite I asked myself if I could get out of this, but before I had a chance to voice my concerns I was gowned up and standing as far back in the operating room as possible.

We were in something called a Charnley theatre, named after a British orthopaedic surgeon who pioneered hip replacements. There was a thick red rectangle and inside this, all the surgeons and nurses were in spacesuits. I was warned that whatever happened I was not to go over the line. The anaesthetist and I were the only people in there not suited up.

The operation wasn't at all as bad as I thought it might be; there wasn't even much blood. I'm unsure if I was disappointed or relieved. The worst part was the bone being sawn through when they dislocated the hip and then removed the worn bits.

I did help at the end of the operation. I was asked to stand just outside the red box with a bit of tape on my finger. This had been cut by the anaesthetist and carefully placed there. She told me it was very important, and I was slightly terrified.

As they finished up, they inserted a drain into the wound. 'Now, Nurse,' said the gas lady. I stepped forward slightly and held out my finger. She took the tape and…fixed the drain in place with it. My work there was done.

Within 48 hours my hip replacement patient was as bright as a button, though another person confined to bed. None of this getting up and racing round 24 hours post-op then. Hell, no. You stayed put and after about four days the bed was turned vertically, very slowly, with two physios and a walking frame waiting to receive you.

So then did the patient go for a walk around? Don't be silly. The person stepped off the bed and got their balance. They stood for a few minutes, and then they were put back to bed, and down it went again. It was like opening a swing bridge when no boats go through and then closing it again. Oh, how times have changed.

It's sad that my lasting memory of male orthopaedic is one of tragedy. It was my finial week on this ward and I was on a late shift. As I walked towards my place of work I could hear a ringing in my ears. No, it wasn't tinnitus, it was the emergency bell, and it was coming from my ward.

Occasionally the big red button did get pushed accidentally, and this was always corrected within seconds. The last thing we wanted was the cardiac arrest team arriving full of adrenaline, since they would relieve all that pent-up energy by shouting at the ward staff. But this wasn't stopping. It went on and on. People raced past me, and I soon joined them, picking up my walk to a run. This is allowed in cases of extreme emergencies, and this looked like one of those.

When I got to the ward all hell seemed to be breaking loose. One of the girls who started with me was sat at the nurses' station crying, people were piled into a cubicle, and I could hear voices shouting for drugs and then 'Clear.' The thud of the defibrillator, and then nothing. 'Right. Start chest compressions again.'

I went to the upset nurse and put my arm around her. 'What's happened?' I asked, though it was obvious. 'It's Raymond. He just collapsed.'

Raymond Taylor was in his mid-twenties and such a nice bloke. Admitted with crush injuries, he had been through the mill. Multiple fractures, many operations. Time in ICU when he was at death's door so many times. But now he was well on the road to recovery. His consultant was even talking about him going home for a weekend soon.

Because he had been injured at work, his company couldn't do enough for him. Whatever he needed, they would get for him. He had a private room, but the only real difference was that he could have visitors any time he pleased. He also had a better menu choice than the other patients, but that apart, he still got the same nursing care as everyone else.

We often would sit with him and talk if it was quiet, and his wife of six months came to see him each day at the same time, one o'clock. We got to know them both well and often said what a lovely couple they made.

'I'm in for a hefty payout for this, Nurse,' he told me one day when I was checking his dressings.

'It will set us up for life. And they've offered me a cushy little number in the office when I'm ready to go back.' Even though Raymond had what today would be called 'life-changing injuries', he was so positive and mostly cheerful. His surgeon was still battling to save one of his legs, but had commented just that week that he didn't think it was a long-term possibility.

After what seemed like hours, the room went very quiet and downcast people trailed out one by one. Our ward sister was crying silently, and Mr Jones, the consultant, was ashen. People didn't die in this ward. It just didn't happen, and everyone was trying to accept the fact that not only had death visited us today, but it had left with a young man who should have had his whole life in front of him.

The place was unnaturally silent. It was eerie. Then Raymond's wife came through the doors with her usual big smile on her face. She stopped in her tracks when she saw our faces and crumpled on the floor screaming. It was one of the worst experiences of my working career.

Two days later, the post-mortem proved our suspicions. Raymond had thrown off a massive fatty clot from one of his many broken bones. It had gone into his lungs and stopped him breathing, and that in turn had stopped his heart.

The fact that nobody could have prevented this didn't make anyone feel any better, and I'm certain that his death affected his surgeon greatly, as not long after he retired.

In the years that followed, I often wondered how his widow was. Did she remarry? Was she happy? I do hope so. But one thing I do know: every person on the ward that day will never forget Raymond.

Chapter 17

Another night, another jumper

I was on my last placement before I took my final exams. I was ready to settle down on this ward and gain experience, so this final hurdle couldn't come quickly enough.

We took our exams in June, but didn't finish our training until the end of August. I think the examining body expected us enrolled nurses to have learned everything we needed to after 22 months, and at the time they were probably right.

One thing did become apparent as my group went into our second year; there wasn't an intake of pupil nurses following us. There were no more enrolled nurses to be trained at this hospital. Indeed, the Department of Health had decided to phase out second level nurses right across the country. We were the last of a type of nurse who didn't want to be a manager, didn't want to run the hospital, but just wanted to look after sick people.

Big mistake? Probably, but EN's were doing more and more duties usually assigned to the RGN's. However, there was a disparity. One day the EN was only good enough to 'shovel shit', and the next day they were expected to run the whole show — on a lower pay scale, to boot.

Strangely, the financial side of the job was seldom talked about, as we were probably the last generation who took the job on because we saw it as a vocation, or at the very least a satisfying work that let you help people when they were at their most vulnerable.

I remember one excellent EN who was in charge of a ward one day when things went horribly wrong. The consultant turned up unexpectedly to do a ward round. There were two very poorly patients and one needed an inhaler. The EN had drawn up the drug ready to administer via a specialised oxygen mask when the consultant appeared, tapping his watch impatiently. The EN turned to a third-year student nurse who was about to take her final exams. 'Do you know how to give this?' she asked, sounding frazzled.

'Of course,' said the student, as she picked up the dish with the syringe in and walked to the patient. Well, I knew how to do that job and had administered the drug many times during my training, so we were all taken aback when the emergency bell started ringing two minutes later. The almost qualified student had given the drug straight into the patient's bloodstream via his canula,(a needle inserted into a vein for the administration of fluids and some drugs) and he was now having cardiac arrhythmias, (irregular rate or/and rhythm at which the heart beats).

The fact that the consultant was on the ward saved the day. He sorted the patient out straight away, and soon he was back to normal. The truth is, though, that the incident wouldn't have happened in the first place if said consultant hadn't thrown the ward routine off-kilter — but that was neither here nor there.

Was there an enquiry into this serious incident? If there was, no one asked me anything about it, and I was in the room when the conversation had taken place between the EN and the student. I did go to help when the emergency bell was activated, I did assist the EN and the consultant in the treatment of the patient, but no one asked me what had happened.

I do know that the EN was hauled over the coals which I consider very unfair. No one talked about being understaffed that day, or the fact that the EN had been lumbered with the responsibility of running the ward, when she shouldn't have been left in sole charge. Oh no, they needed a scapegoat and she was it.

It did make me wonder if doing the EN course had been such a good idea, especially as we were apparently no longer worth training. And I'm sure that man who interviewed me must have known this when he told me I wasn't up to doing the RGN training — the git!

***

I digress. Back to nights.

I was back on men's surgical again for the next eight weeks. Because I had now gained confidence and knew the ward this held no fears for me. Just as with my nights on medical, I felt comfortable here.

We had plenty of staff which I know is usual these days, but don't forget, student nurses and pupil nurses were on the duty rota then. We got paid a salary, and as such we were expected to work the same shifts as everyone else.

Also, this was not a massive hospital and not all the wards were training wards. Due to this my nights on men's surgical saw about 5 learners and one EN who was in charge, with a staff nurse running between two wards as the person who was really in charge as a legal requirement. As the EN got moved most nights onto a busier ward, the staff nurse was needed more than usual. She had to do drugs for two wards and oversee anything that a trained nurse had to do, which was most things.

Fortunately, this group of nurses looking after the patients were level-headed and quite capable of handling most eventualities, which was just as well considering what the night had in store.

Again, nights tended to be quiet, and once the lights went out about eleven, we just had to make sure drains were draining, drips were dripping, and dressings were not soaked in blood. Simple.

We did get the odd emergency that usually came straight from theatre, but we always had plenty of notice, and yes, we always had a bed available. I can't quite understand this compared to today.

We kept people in longer, there wasn't any MRSA and we always found a bed for emergencies. Something has gone wrong somewhere, but I'd like someone to explain this to me.

There was an admission going on that evening while we were given the handover by the day staff.

'His name is Jacob,' the staff nurse told us. 'He's in with a head injury and possibly a partly detached right retina. So, half-hourly neuro obs and bed rest. Oh, and by the way his surname is Waverly. His father is Mr Waverly, the heart surgeon.' This meant nothing to me, and as this man didn't even work at our hospital, I wasn't that impressed at all.

When we came out of the office a woman in tears came out of a cubicle. 'Bye honeybunny, Mummy will be back first thing in the morning.' With a sniff, she turned to us. 'You will look after him, won't you? He's pretending he's tough, but he's not. He's just my scared little boy.'

We smiled and assured Mrs Waverly that her honeybunny would get the best of care, and yes, we would phone her if there was any change, and yes, she could phone us if she was worried, and of course we would make him some warm milk to help him sleep.

Finally, she left and one of the nurses went in to see how this little lad was, though I was sure the staff nurse had said in the report that he was eighteen. Maybe I'd misheard, but we seldom took anyone under fifteen on this adult ward.

Our colleague came out and reported to us that the 'little boy' was in fact six foot three, weighed fifteen stone, and had a mouth like a sewer. 'This is going to be a very long shift,' she said quietly, and she was to be proved right.

As we settled down for the night around the nursing station, I got my knitting out. Yes, all right, I should have been revising as some of my colleagues were, but if I started reading, I just fell asleep. I still do. But knitting a jumper for one of my children kept me focused. I could put it down at a moment's notice and rush off to see to a patient, and then pick it back up again and continue without too many holes appearing, or ventilation as I like to call them.

'Nurse,' came the call from the cubicle behind us.

'I'll go,' volunteered a colleague. She went into his room. We could hear raised voices and the nurse trying to placate a very agitated Jacob. Finally she emerged and dropped into her seat. 'He wants to go for a walk. Said he needs a cig.'

'What did you say?' I asked.

'I told him he's not well and he needs to rest. He got back into bed and told me to fuck off.'

'Charming!'

'I don't suppose it's his fault. He probably isn't usually like this. It will be the head injury. Anyway, before I came out I did his obs and they were okay.'

And so it continued. We would take it in turns to try and mollify Jacob, get him to lie still, and do his observations as best way we could.

I was glad when my meal break came around. Normally I took sandwiches and stayed on the ward, but tonight I couldn't wait to get away from Jacob and his uncalled-for behaviour. We were all giving him the benefit of the doubt, but I wasn't convinced that his nastiness was all down to his head injury.

As I walked back down the corridor I heard my name called, and turned to see Babs from my training group running after me. 'You on a break?'

I nodded and she fell in step with me. 'What's all the commotion on your ward?'

I explained about our VIP guest and mentioned that his father was a heart surgeon.

'Oh yes, I've heard of him. Apparently he's brilliant but very scary.'

'Well, his son is a pain in the arse. How's your shift?'

'We have a terminally ill lady in one of our cubicles. She's only 39 with 2 children and she has CA (cancer) of the pancreas. Doesn't seem to matter what we give to her, she's rolling round in agony. It's awful.'

This woman was the same age as me, and I also had 2 children. That made me think, and I went back to the ward after my break with a different mindset. Putting up with Jacob was nothing compared to what was going on next door.

Two other nurses went off for their breaks when I got back, and all was quiet. I sat down and picked up my knitting again.

'Nurse!!!!'

'I'll go,' said Debbie, a pretty little student nurse who had just gone into her second year. She was kind, gentle and would do anything asked of her without complaint. She hadn't said a word about our awkward boy racer who, as it turned out, had come off a quad bike on his friend's farm, and wasn't wearing any protective headgear. After all, that wouldn't have looked cool.

Debbie went in and closed the door only to emerge a few minutes later in tears. 'What's wrong?' I asked.

'He won't get back into bed, and he…'

'He what?'

'He touched me, and said I'd be a good f…' She couldn't bring herself to say the word.

'RIGHT!' I was past angry. I threw my knitting down and pushed my cardigan sleeves up. This meant war.

Jacob was sitting on the edge of his bed peeing on the floor. He looked at me and smiled. I grabbed the sheet lying in a heap on the bed and threw it on the floor to soak up the mess. 'Bed, now, you little shit!'

If I was going for the shock treatment it was working. He looked genuinely surprised, but quickly rallied. He stood up. 'Or what?' he asked, with just a bit more threat in his voice than there had been in mine.

I took hold of his pyjama top and screwed it up tightly pulling him close to me, 'or I'll slap your silly face. Then I'll fill in a report of sexual abuse, and then I'll get the police to interview you.'

'What? I didn't touch you.' Now, at last, he sounded frightened.

'Not me, you prat, that pretty nurse that was in with you a moment ago.'

'It was just a joke,' he stammered.

'Well, she's not laughing. Now, get into bed and stay there.'

'You can't treat me like this. Do you know who my father is? I'll tell him all about you!'

'Don't bother, I'll be telling him first.' And I stormed out of the room, leaving him with no chance of a comeback.

'So that's my nursing career down the drain before I've even done my final exams,' I said as I sat back down again.

'You were wonderful,' said the other girls, but all I could see was Jacob's dad tearing me into tiny strips for threatening his son, and demanding my immediate dismissal. However, we didn't hear another peep out of the troublemaker, so maybe it had been worth it.

Morning came a-calling and as the day staff took the report. I felt quite sick about what might transpire when they heard about my behaviour, though the nurse giving the report told me not to worry.

She came out of the office and winked at me. I'd got away with it.

But no. Just at that moment a very smartly-dressed man walked onto the ward. There was no doubt that this was Jacob's father. He nodded at us. 'Good morning.'

I could have just gone off the ward, I could, but I didn't. 'Mr Waverly?'

'Yes.'

'I'm one of the nurses that looked after your son last night.'

'And was there a problem, Nurse?'

'Yes, I'm afraid there was. You see, Jacob was rather rude to, well, all of us actually, and then he touched one of the nurses, and I'm sorry but I lost my temper and shouted at him.'

The man stared at me, but his facial expression didn't alter at all. Then he said, 'Thank you, Nurse, I'll see to this.' He went past me into the room and slowly shut the door. But we all heard what was said in there. 'Wake up Jacob, you little shit. You've got some explaining to do and a lot of apologies to make.'

I didn't see Jacob again since he was transferred later that day to another hospital which came with the word 'private' before it. Also, the 'incident' was never mentioned again, and we came on duty that night to find the biggest box of chocolates known to man. I swear you probably could have seen it from outer space. But it was the card that came with it which made us all smile.

'Thank you for your patience with me. I didn't deserve it.' It was signed: 'The Little Shit'!

Chapter 18

Almost there

The exam came and went, and to be honest it was a bit of an anti-climax in the end. We did, though, have a highlight during one of our study days leading up to the big event, and that was a pirate video of ET. Our tutor must have had other things to do that morning, so he came into the classroom and told us this was our revision on how to deal with a cardiac arrest. If you haven't seen ET you won't understand this reference, and if you haven't seen ET, shame on you. Watch it at once!

I was given my final ward before I hopefully qualified, and this was once again men's surgical. It felt like an old friend by now, and I was more than happy to stay there until all my practical hours were completed.

I noticed I was treated slightly different now that I had taken my finals. Though I couldn't do certain things like give the ward report, take a consultant's round or generally be in charge, I was treated for most of the time as a qualified member of staff, which was great, and did my self-confidence good. I would have liked nothing more than to have stayed on this ward with a contract, but that wasn't going to happen. They had their full quota of staff and as it was such a nice ward to work on, especially since the scary sister had gone off to have a baby, there was a queue of nurses who would have wrestled me to the ground in their attempt to secure a job on men's surgical.

When I did my last stint in that ward we had two nurses who were training at the local psychiatric hospital; one male, one female. They were obliged to do six months in a general hospital to broaden their nursing experience, as people with mental health issues could have other things wrong with them, so it was good practice that the staff had a basic understanding of physical illness and its manifestations.

The male nurse was very nice and tried hard to learn, but it was obvious that he was out of his comfort zone, and had to be told frequently that he needed to 'get on'. He would often pull up a chair and chat to the patients, while all around him there would be a whirlwind of activity that he didn't seem to be aware of. He wasn't lazy, just used to talking to his patients — a lot!

We had a big theatre list one day, and I asked him to help me get one gentleman ready to go to for his operation. He was great, and together we had all the checklist done and dusted quickly and efficiently. There was just one more man to go down for his surgery and I asked the nurse if he could cope with it on his own. 'It's easy, you do what we have just done. Checklist, right patient, right notes, right armband, check the operation site has been shaved, false teeth out, or anything else that's false. The staff nurse will give him his pre-med in a minute, then just gown him up and Bob's your uncle.'

He seemed keen to do that, and I went to do a dressing in the clinical room. This was for one of our patients who had had surgery with us several weeks before, and his wound just wouldn't heal properly. Eventually he was allowed home, but came to the ward each day to have his dressing done and so that we could keep an eye on him and adjust his treatment as necessary.

The EN was helping me as it was quite a marathon doing this task, and we were gowned up and had masks on when we heard a tap at the door.

'Yes?' called the EN.

Our male nurse popped his head around the door, 'Sorry, but I can't find any theatre gowns.'

'Try women's surgical,' said the EN, without looking away from her task.

'Okay. Thanks.'

We had just about finished when one of the theatre porters came in without knocking. 'Hey, come and look at this!' He disappeared, and we went to see what he considered so important he needed to barge into a clean dressing area.

Our patient was on the trolley looking suitably sedated, but the second theatre porter was laughing and our male nurse was looking uncomfortable. 'I didn't know,' he said defensively.

'What's wrong?' I asked. Nothing seemed out of place to me. The first porter peeled back the blanket covering the patient. 'Oh my God.'

'Exactly,' said the porter, and sniggered. 'I think we're being a bit presumptuous. He's not even had his op yet!'

The gentlemen on the trolley had a lovely gown on. It had frills around the neck and an embroidered cross midway down, with lace about the cuffs. Yes, you've guessed it, it was a shroud.

The EN found a theatre gown and we did a quick change there and then in the middle of the ward. It was like getting into your swimming gear at the beach under a towel, but soon the patient was on his way to theatre, not the mortuary.

To be fair to the lad, he had never had to lay out a dead person so wouldn't have known what a shroud should look like. He just supposed that the ladies had nicer theatre gowns than the men.

Bless him.

The female part of this twosome was worldly-wise and a real asset to any department. She had started her general training at one point, and then left feeling it wasn't what she wanted to do. Now older and with more life experience, she had decided on mental health training, and I saw on several occasions that she suited it very well.

The first time her experience and training came to light was when we had a man admitted with renal colic. This is when you get urinary stones blocking part of the tubes from where you pee. It can be, and usually is, an excruciating pain.

One of my nursing friends collapsed with renal colic while at work. She was admitted to female surgery and after a hefty dose of morphine managed a very unnatural, but nevertheless restful sleep. She was woken early the next day by two happy-clappy nurses who encouraged her to sit in the chair while they straightened her bed.

'Can't you just leave me?' she pleaded.

'Now, all we want to do is make you comfortable. So just pop into this armchair and we will sort you out.'

'No, really. I'm fine. I just want to lie still and go back to sleep.'

'Come on, the sooner you get out the sooner you can get back in again.'

'But I really don't feel well.'

'Everyone here isn't well,' said the nurse with a smile, as she took my friend's arm to assist her out of her bed. At the point, my friend vomited copious amounts of noxious stomach contents all over the nurse who had hold of her, and then fainted. That nurse sustained a sprained wrist trying to stop her patient's fall and smelt as she had just emerged from a sewer for the rest of the day.

When my friend was over this and back at work, she told me it was the worst pain she had ever had, including the birth of her three children. She had also learned to listen to her patients, and she hoped she would be more understanding after her experience.

Meanwhile, back to our patient. He was put in a side ward as, apart from when he was curled in a ball on his bed screaming for painkillers, he was ambulant and self-caring. He had a urinary bottle by his bed and was under strict instructions to use it and then let one of the staff know. Then we took it off to the sluice where it was sieved to see if he had passed any stones and tested for anything that shouldn't be there. We were looking for blood, as it was common to see this in the urine of patients suffering renal colic. Sure enough, now and again we found blood. After one particularly bad episode of pain, when he finally managed to pass urine, we also found a tiny piece of grit. I felt sorry for him, and he was due to go for a scan on the Monday after being admitted late Friday with this awful problem. Strong pain relief was all we could do for him, and encourage him to drink plenty of fluids.

It was Monday morning when fate took a hand in the guise of our female psychiatric student nurse who had just had two days off. After handover she picked up one patient's notes and examined them carefully, then asked me to go to his room with her. This was the renal colic guy.

When we got there he was missing, having probably gone for a smoke. 'Shut the door,' she said in a whisper. I shrugged and did what I'd been told. Quickly and carefully she started to go

through the things in his bedside locker.

'You can't do that!' To say I was shocked was putting it mildly. But as these words left my lips, she pulled out a matchbox. In the box were several pieces of grit in various sizes, and some pins. She smiled as she showed this to me. 'Got ye,' she said to herself.

Just then the patient came into his room, took one look at us and his whole demeanour changed. 'Oh, fucking hell, what are you doing here?'

'Well well, we meet again, Michael. Fancy seeing you here.'

'Who's Michael? He's not called Michael!'

'Oh yes he is.'

85

I'll give you a short version of what was going on. Michael was a known drug addict and had been in and out of the mental institution where this nurse worked many times. His latest scam was to go around to different A&Es late on Friday showing signs and symptoms of renal colic, knowing that he would have to wait all weekend for a scan to prove if his diagnosis was correct. In the interim he would be offered class A drugs free via the NHS.

Using the matchbox, now and again he would prick his finger and squeeze a little blood into his urine, and when the need arose, he would also add another ingredient, grit just to give his pee that extra zing. Once sussed, he quickly left without the need of the police being called and we all, except the one nurse that really knew him, felt very foolish and used.

***

Results day came around. I held the brown envelope in my hand for a while, then took a deep breath and tore it open. I'd passed. I was delighted, but honestly, but I would have been very surprised and disappointed if I had failed.

Putting in the hours on the wards was 80% of what we needed to do. The rest was the theory, which I had enjoyed learning, and it had stayed where it needed to stay; in my head.

All my group passed (only two people had dropped out during the two years), and I was pleased for every one of them.

We had a presentation night at the psychiatric hospital and were given our hospital certificate and badges. Then we had to fill in a form and pay our registration fee, which would allow us to be entered on the second part of the qualified nurses register, a one-off, lifetime registration payment we were told, (they lied) and then we were free to apply for jobs. And that's where the problems started.

Chapter 19

A job's a job (or is it?)

The pickings were meagre, to say the least. There were eighteen of us applying for twelve jobs, and eleven of those were on the geriatric wards. The only position that wasn't working directly with the elderly was in theatre. No one who had worked there as a pupil wanted it, and the people who hadn't worked there wanted it even less. It wasn't that theatre was a horrible place to work, it was just an acquired taste. After all, as state enrolled nurses we had trained to look after sick people, and preferably those that were awake. All this technical stuff scared us normal nurses to death.

We said goodbye to a few colleagues as they spread their wings and went further afield. Did I envy them? Yes, just a bit.

I applied for a post at something called 'The Geriatric Day Hospital' along with five other candidates. There were two positions and I was one of the successful applicants. Now if I'm brutally honest, I didn't want to make looking after old people my life's work. Old people smell, are grumpy and at some point, they go and die on you (I can say this now I'm old myself). However, this job had more positives than negatives. It was Monday to Friday, nine to five. No bank holidays, no late shift, no weekends. I was more than pleased to secure this cushy number. I was grateful that I had got a job, any job, and that it had what I considered to be normal working hours. This was a rarity in nursing then, and still is to some extent.

The Day Hospital catered for the elderly walking ill. About twenty patients came in each morning by ambulance, which was a glorified minibus, and stayed the day. While they were in our care they saw the doctor, had tests, did physio, saw the chiropodist, and could even have a bath and get their hair washed. The dietitian would visit and give people menus to follow, which they promptly ignored. We saw around ninety different patients a week, and a few that came to us twice a week, but that was not encouraged.

There was a staff of seven on the unit. Starting at the top: the sister in charge, a staff nurse, three ENs, an auxiliary nurse and finally a ward clerk. Oh, and the most important member of the team, Margaret the cleaner. I don't say this tongue in cheek. She kept the place clean and she talked to the patients, who told her things they wouldn't tell the nursing staff. She made us tea when we were flagging, had the consultant eating out of her hand, and all with a smile and never a complaint.

Once, just once, someone made the mistake of calling her 'just the cleaner', and compounded their heinous statement by adding, 'I feel sorry for her. She must need the money — after all, who'd want to be a cleaner?'

We all gasped. 'I'll have you know she is the backbone of this place,' one of my colleagues said indignantly.

Margaret heard this exchange. 'I just do it to get myself out of the house,' she remarked as she tidied away the lunch things. They didn't believe her, but quite frankly she didn't give a fig.

What they didn't know was that Margaret could have bought and sold most of them. She came to work in a brand-new Mercedes and holidayed in the Seychelles. And she did indeed do the job to get her out of the house. The hours suited her, as did the job. I admired and respected that woman, and hoped one day I would be like her and drive a new Mercedes. Shallow, I know.

I soon slipped into the routine of working life at the Day Hospital, and to say it didn't tax one's nursing skills would be an accurate statement. To do what we did then, the place only needed two qualified nurses and three or four nursing auxiliaries now. I soon started to become bored and, in all honesty, I can only recall two incidents from my time there, the rest being mundane and routine. One of these things was the day I gave the wrong person the wrong medication. But more about that later.

Firstly, John Smith. Mr Smith came to us as most of our patients did, via a GP referral. He was an eighty-something bachelor, about 6 feet 2 inches, very lean and pale. He looked undernourished, and the referral was for weight loss, querying the cause.

I took him into the office with tea and biscuits as a bribe and started his assessment. I did his weight and height. 'I might have lost a few ponds, but I don't do anything these days, so I'm not hungry,' he said when I told him he was underweight. Fair statement! His blood pressure was a tad on the low side and his pulse was slightly raised. But mentally he was sharp as a pin and didn't have any memory issues, so that was a box we could tick.

'And how have you been in yourself?' I asked.

'A bit tired, and I have dizzy spells now and again.'

'Okay. That might be a drop in your blood pressure when you go from sitting to standing. Tell you what, I'll do your BP in the chair and then I'll check it again when you stand up.'

We did this, but there was no drop in his pressure, so back to the old drawing board. 'Any other symptoms?'

'Well, I get a bit breathless when I go upstairs. And the old ticker goes like the clappers. But what can you expect at my age?'

When I asked to see John's medication, he produced one small bottle of iron tablets. 'Where are the rest?' I asked.

89

'That's all. And I only got them because my doctor thought I might be a bit anaemic.'

'And do you take then?' I asked, eyeing the almost-full bottle.

'Not really. I don't like taking tablets.'

Later that morning our registrar did a clinic at which I assisted, and he saw John Smith first. After a thorough examination, he declared John had a fast pulse and a low BP. 'Nurse tells me your doctor gave you iron tablets, but you don't take them.'

'They bung me up,' he whispered, so as not to embarrass me.

'I'd like to run a few routine tests on you, Mr Smith. Then I'll see you next week with the results and we can take it from there.'

'Oh, I've got to come back next week then?' He did not sound pleased at this prospect.

'Yes, if you don't mind.'

'Don't suppose I'll have to mind.'

John was in a much better mood after a hearty lunch, and was then whisked off in an ambulance to the main building with our axillary to have an ECG and some routine blood tests. That was the other thing about the Day Hospital. We were an outpost, so far away from the main hospital that we required transport for our patients when they needed to go anywhere else within the grounds.

He returned just as the ambulances were arriving to take our flock home, and I was helping him with his coat when the ward clerk came into the room and waved to me. 'It's the lab on the phone. They want to speak to a nurse.'

This was unusual as our clerk was more than capable of taking down test results, so I did wonder why suddenly they wanted a real nurse to talk to. 'Hello, Nurse Bissett.'

'Hello, nurse. It's Kevin here. Kevin from the lab.' We all knew Kevin. He was a very clever biochemist, but when he spoke it was slowly, and monotone. No feeling at all.

'Hello, Kevin. What can I do for you today?'

'Mr John Smith...'

'Yes?'

'Is he still with you?'

'Just about. He's getting on the ambulance as we speak.'

'Right. Under his own steam? Not on a trolley or in a wheel-chair?'

'No, why?'

'Well, when I asked if he was still with you, I meant is he still alive.'

'What?'

'He has no right to be breathing, let alone getting on an ambulance. I've seen better Hb when we've done tests on corpses. His haemoglobin is 3.5!' The normal level for a man is 13-18.

'WHAT?'

'I said —'

'I know what you said. Are you serious?'

'When am I not serious?'

This was very true. Kevin didn't do funny. He did sarcastic very well, but not funny.

We extracted Mr Smith from the jaws of the ambulance in the nick of time, though he did grip onto the handrail for longer than necessary, and I thought for one terrible moment that he was going to refuse to be escorted back into the building.

He was admitted straight away and given three units of blood, after which he felt considerably better. He had a further three units later in the week, by which time the doctors had done further investigations and discovered that he had a duodenal ulcer which was bleeding very slowly. So slowly that the effects were insidious, and John's had just become used to the lack of oxygen circulating in his body, and coped with it.

John Smith made a complete recovery and lived on for many more healthy years. It's nice to save a life now and again.

**

After 18 months of this routine, him indoors started to get a tad vexed with my constant whinging of 'What did I do two years' training for, trained monkeys could do my job,' etc, etc.

'Don't moan. Do something about it!'

With this I found myself back in the School of Nursing enquiring about doing a further two years of training to bring me up to an RGN. I was somewhat put out when the new head of nursing training said I had to prove I could do further study. When I pointed out that I had seven GCE O Levels and that you still only needed three to apply to do the 3-year course, and that I had spent 2 years training to be an EN, he simply said, 'Go to night school and do another qualification. Then come back and we will talk again.'

I got pregnant instead. That will show him, I thought!

I was very pregnant and getting ready to leave to have my third baby when the incident happened. At this hospital enrolled nurses were not allowed to do the drugs round on their own. They could help, but not take the drugs trolley off for a little run without an RGN driving it. Suddenly someone decided that if an EN was assessed on medicines they too could hold the keys. I didn't bother as I was leaving, and at that point didn't know when I would be back, and all the rules would probably have changed again by then.

'Can you do the drugs for me, please?' sister asked, as she got ready to go to a meeting.

'Me?' I said, looking round to see if she was speaking to somebody behind me.

'Yes, you.' She dangled the drugs keys in front of me like a temptress.

'But I can't. I haven't done the medicine assessment yet.'

'And whose fault is that? You've had plenty of opportunities.' She put the keys in my hand. 'Come on, there isn't much to it here. Just a few painkillers and one or two antibiotics.' With that she left, and I didn't seem to have a further say on the matter.

I shouldn't have done them. I should have had the courage of my convictions. But I wanted to please everyone, and not cause problems.

The drugs trolley had in it the patients' tablets, which they were instructed to bring with them on each visit if they might need to have them during their stay with us. As I went around the day room I went to each person, asked them their name, and gave them their pills.

This was going fine until I asked Gladys if she wanted her travel sickness tablets. 'What?' she shouted with her hand behind her ear.

'Your tablets, Gladys.' I handed them to her, and she promptly swallowed them. As this happened I realised my awful mistake. It was the wrong Gladys. We had two ladies with the same Christian name on that day.

I felt myself go hot and cold, and then hot again. I visualised Gladys dropping dead in front of me, and me being charged with manslaughter. Instead of maternity leave, I'd be doing porridge. As I was playing out this awful scenario in my head the auxiliary came up to me. 'Are you okay? You've gone very pale. You're not in labour, are you?' She gave me a friendly punch on the arm and laughed. I told her what had happened, and she just smiled. 'It's only a travel sickness tablets for God's sake. No one's going to run you out of town for that.'

Sister had a different opinion. When I told her she sucked air in through her teeth. 'This is very serious,' she said, in a voice which matched her expression.

'Is it? Well yes, I know it's not good, but I did say I hadn't done the assessment.'

Sister looked pensive. She wasn't impressed. I tried not to look upset and my defence just made things worse. She went slightly red in the face. Not a good sign. 'Are you saying this is my fault, nurse?'

'No, but...'

'Good. I will fill in an incident form. You write down exactly what happened, and then I'll get a doctor to countersign the form and send it to the matron.'

By this time I was almost in tears. I had two weeks to go before I left to have my baby, and now I would be finishing with a permanent mark on my record. This could have implications if and when I started looking for nursing jobs in the future, but at that moment I would have quite happily have given up my nursing career for good.

I went and sat on my own in the treatment room and scribbled down my account of what had happened, tears streaming down my face. When I had finished, I went into sister's office and almost threw the piece of paper at her. She just gave me a stony look. 'You can go now, nurse, but I expect matron will need to see you tomorrow.'

I had a sleepless night and felt even more sick than my usual morning sickness as I made my way to work the following day. We took a report first thing in the morning and nothing was mentioned about my misdemeanour, though everyone knew what had happened.

About an hour later most of the patients had arrived and our registrar turned up to do his clinic.

He was a middle-aged man who always looked sad. We suspected he had been overlooked for a post as a consultant quite a few times, but we didn't know why. He hardly ever smiled, but he was a good doctor and I liked him.

The nurses had a competition that if we made him smile, we got first pick of the biscuits at coffee time, but it didn't happen that often. Sister picked up the incident form and disappeared into the doctor's room with him, firmly shutting the door behind her.

I stood on the corridor waiting for her to come out, which she did after about five minutes, not looking best pleased, and as she walked towards her office, I could see her screwing up the form in her hands.

I popped my head into the doctor's room, and he looked at me. 'Don't worry, this won't go any further. I'm not signing that!' He pointed after sister. 'It's ridiculous.'

'Thank you' was all I could manage.

I found out later that day that the doctor had said the day hospital didn't have a safe protocol for the administration of drugs, and that all patients needed to have an ID bracelet on for their stay to make it feasible. I never did find out if this policy was implemented as I went off sick the next day with high blood pressure. I wonder why that was?

PART THREE
1986-1991

Chapter 20

A sense of direction

Fast forward twelve months. I was sitting on the floor with my one-year-old, looking at the Situations Vacant page of the local newspaper, while my son tried to eat said paper.

I had discovered quite quickly in life that I get bored easily. I missed going out to work and I especially missed the money. But I didn't think that going back to nursing was going to be feasible with three children at home to look after, until an advert shot off the page and hit me straight in the eye.

'Enrolled Nurses wanted for the evening service. Driving licence and the use of a car essential.'

I was an enrolled nurse, tick, I could drive, tick, and I could use the car at night, tick. Him indoors could come home after a long shift, make his own tea, put the kids to bed, wash the dishes and then relax. He wouldn't mind, would he?

But as I tried to hook the chewed-up newspaper out of my adorable child's mouth I wondered if it was a bit too soon. At that precise moment my son sneezed straight into my face and pebble-dashed me. No, it wasn't too soon at all!

That was July, and now, at the beginning of September, I was standing in the District Nurse's office at 6 pm clad head-to-foot in green. Green hat, green dress, green cardigan, green coat and the only thing not green was my black tights, which went very well with the lovely nurses' bag that hung on my shoulder.

I looked like something between the Jolly Green Giant and crew for Aer Lingus.

The sister in charge introduced me to the rest of the team and then we had a quick report. Most of the patients were regulars and needed the same care each evening, hence the quick report. When someone new came onto the list we were given more details and if anything changed in someone's life we were told that as well; most of the time, that is.

The shift was 6-10 pm and there were two teams. We worked opposite each other and both teams did seven evenings a fortnight.

The patients that we went to see lived all around the town, so this made for a great deal of driving. A district nurse on days at that time would be based with GP's and so their patch was quite small, but we had everyone from everywhere.

Each team had one RGN, six ENs and four auxiliaries. The auxiliaries were brilliant but limited on what they could do. Sometimes we went out in pairs but usually we worked alone, and we were given radios to keep in touch with each other.

The first seven evenings were a doddle as I was always with another trained nurse who would drive and show me the ropes. It was the second lot of evenings when I started having a problem; I constantly got lost. It hadn't been mentioned that to do this job you needed a good sense of direction. If it had, I might not have applied in the first place. I failed my Tracker badge in Girl Guides for a very good reason; I can never find a place unless I've been there several times in the daylight. I was rubbish at navigating my way around then and I still am now, but the big differences today are mobile phones and satnavs.

I was late finishing almost every evening because of this, not making my way home at nine like some of the girls who knew not only the patients back to front, but all the rat runs and short cuts. It became a joke after a while, and even I had to laugh at some of the places I ended up at. But as my mistakes meant I was getting home regularly after eleven it soon lost its humour and became a trial.

Eventually I got better at navigating, and made a point the following summer, with its light nights, of memorising routes which would help me once winter was with us again. I did love the job, however, and worked with a fabulous set of girls who all supported each other.

I was almost finished one evening when the radio crackled asking me if I were free to go to a gentleman who was terminally ill and needed an injection for pain. This was not far from where I lived, and when the sister told me I could then go home and bring my radio back the next day I was happy. It was 9.30 pm, so that meant for once I would get home on time.

I found the address quite easily and the patient's neighbour let me in. The sick man was in his front room on a bed under the window. The place was dark and depressing, and the gentleman was very ill indeed. I checked the documentation and drew up the drug. He was in a great deal of pain and I sat with him until the morphine started to take effect.

Outside the room, the lady who had let me in and I spoke in hushed tones. 'Hasn't he got anyone that can sit with him?' I asked.

'Well, he has children, but they won't have anything to do with him.'

'But why? He's at death's door.'

'Not my place to say.' But she did anyway. 'He's been a wicked man. Not sure what happened, but his children hate him. I got in touch with one of them, and when I told her he was dying, she just said "Good." and closed the door in my face.'

'I don't like leaving him,' I said, looking back towards the house.

She patted my arm, 'Don't worry, pet. I'll sit with him a bit longer. I'm sure you've got others to see to. You're all angels in my eyes.'

I did get home on time that night, though I didn't appreciate it, as my thought kept going back to the sad little man lying in that room. What could have been so bad for his family to treat him like that? But that's not for me to ask.

I wasn't surprised to find out the next day that he had died in the early hours of the morning, and I was relieved to be told his neighbour was with him at the end.

The following week I saw the complete opposite of the sad tale I'd witnessed with the man whose family had disowned him. This was Lilian, who was very old, and dying of nothing more than being very old. She was in a large bed in a small downstairs room when I went to see her, surrounded by three of her many daughters. The room was quiet and had subdued lighting, with scented candles burning and soothing music playing softly.

The daughters in attendance that evening told me the night shift would be taking over soon, that they never left her, and there were always at least two of them there at any one time. They had cared for this lady when she became bedridden; washing her, feeding her, cleaning her, but most of all, being with her.

'You're doing a wonderful job,' I said, as I squeezed past one of them to get to the head of the bed and check Lilian's pulse.

'Why wouldn't we? No one except family know the sacrifices our mum made for us.'

I nodded, but I was more concerned about the old lady's breathing which was irregular and laboured.

'She's going downhill fast, isn't she Nurse?'

I could neither deny nor confirm this, having never seen this lady before. 'She is very poorly,' was all I could honestly say in truth, but she was showing signs that her body had started to shut down. She was also distressed, and I guessed in pain, so I drew up her injection, which was the reason I had called.

I was just hovering with the syringe over her right buttock, having got her daughters to turn her for me, when the one nearest to me said, 'This will kill her, then?'

I stopped, put down the syringe, and took a deep breath. 'What do you mean, exactly?'

'Well, morphine depresses the respiratory center in the brain, and her breathing is not good anyway, so will this finish her off?'

I didn't know what to say, because her conclusion could well be true. I cleared my throat. 'Well, that might happen, but it might happen even if I don't give her the injection. Do you want me to hold off and request the night nurses come in? Though I can't give you a time for that.'

'Good God, no. We don't want her suffering. No, go ahead and give her the injection nurse.'

I was hoping they would say they would wait, but this poor lady was obviously in pain, so I gave her the drug and we got her comfortable.

One of the daughters saw me out. 'Thank you, nurse. Do you think I should get the rest of my sisters round?'

'I think that might be a good idea. I don't think she has long now,' I said in my best 'be brave' voice.

I went back to the office to drop off my radio and told my boss all about my visit. She mollified me by saying they were a lovely family and just wanted their mother to be at peace. 'Believe me, if she goes tonight it will be a blessing for them all.'

Three weeks later that lady was still going — I won't say strong, but she died peacefully with her adoring family around her four weeks after my visit. So, what do I know?

***

I think I would have stayed with the evening service a good many more years if it hadn't been for the attack. Not on any of our staff, but on a young woman walking home alone at 11 pm who was beaten up. It was in an area we visited quite often, and the problem there was that you had to park your car and then walk through trees and dark passageways to get to the person you were going to see.

It freaked us all out, and I went to see the manager and asked if we could work in pairs in that area for safety reasons. She said no. 'You knew what the job involved when you took it on,' was her response as she dismissed me. The sister in charge did try to either give us any visits to that area early in our shift, or send us out in twos, but it depended on many variables and so often nurses were going alone to such places at ten in the evening.

It wasn't that area that finally saw me looking for another job, but a similar layout of housing. I parked my car and tried to find the flat I'd been sent to with no luck. The way the buildings were numbered just didn't make any sense to me and I was about to go back to the car when I saw a policeman. I ran to him. 'Hi, can you tell me where this is?' I said, showing him my diary with the address in it.

'Yes. Go down that path there and it's under the subway.'

I looked horrified. 'It's a bit dark for a nurse on her own,' I said, looking at him hopefully.

'Too right it is, so don't waste time.' With that he turned around and walked quickly away. My knight in shining armor. Yes, right!

I went in the direction he had indicated, and then heard someone behind me. I froze. I could feel my legs starting to shake, so I walked as quickly as I could.

A whistle, low and threatening, came from beside me. I wanted to run, but I didn't think I could. I was just coming to the subway when...

'Boo!'

I screamed, very loud.

'Oops sorry, you're not Martine.'

'What? Who?' My heart was thumping in my chest as a young man stood before me, the worse for the alcohol he had consumed.

'Martine. I thought you were my bird.'

'Oh, and your 'bird' dresses up like a district nurse does she.' I shouted as my fear evaporated and anger took hold.

'I wish,' he said with a smirk on his face. Then he looked at my horrified expression, 'no, but it's dark.'

'No shit, Sherlock! You IDIOT.' With that, I walked quickly away and eventually found the flat I was looking for.

The whole episode unnerved me more than I was willing to admit, and all I could think was that he could have attacked me. I could have ended up in hospital, or even worse the morgue.

Thus I started my search for my next job. Hopefully, one that would be safer.

Chapter 21

A private affair

I always said I wouldn't work in private medicine, being a socialist, and I believe that we should all have the same health-care regardless of our financial situation, but this was too good to pass up.

A bright new shiny all-singing all-dancing hospital had opened on the edge of town, and they wanted bright new shiny all-singing all-dancing staff to run it. I went for an interview and was offered two nights each week, starting at 8 pm and finishing at 8 am. My principles went out of the window and I jumped at the chance. After all, sleep is vastly over-rated.

We were dressed in white from head to foot, and even though I voiced a concern that some poor soul, high on morphine, might think we were ghosts at two in the morning I just got 'a look' from management. To be honest no one ever did think that except for a few of the staff, but that was from lack of sleep, not class A drugs. I hoped.

The first month was a breeze with the hospital slowly building up its reputation and advertising its existence. We had plenty of night staff and not many patients, and even as things progressed and we became very busy it was still a dream to work there. Though at times, when I didn't get enough sleep, the reality and the subconscious did get a little confused, so 'dream job' was an apt description.

We were treated well and respected for our professional expertise by management. However, the hospital did change hands a few times over the years and not always for the better.

We were seeing patients for elective surgery only at first, so no dramatic life-threatening emergencies were being rushed into us in the middle of the night.

Once on duty we got down to real nursing straight away, as the evening drink was done by the housekeeper.

This meant drugs round, observations and by 11.30 everyone was settled for a good rest, including the staff. Only joking, though as we were allowed a one-hour break, and had nowhere to spend it, we took it in turns to find an empty room and put our feet up, eat our supper, watch TV on very low, read, knit or whatever one did to make their break relaxing.

Did we ever nod off? Sometimes. But our colleagues would make sure we didn't go over our hour, and it was always understood that if needed we would be there without hesitation.

Ninety-five per cent of our patients were covered by private medical insurance, mostly through their work. Because of this we saw people from all walks of life, but some of them did think they were better than the rest of us and became very demanding.

One gentleman took great pleasure in telling anyone that would listen about his new car, his new house, his fantastic holiday, and on it went. 'Don't think I'll have the soup; this dressing gown is pure silk. It cost £200.' But one night when we were especially busy, his constant demand for attention wore a bit thin.

It was a perfect storm in nursing. We had not one but two staff call in sick at the last minute, and one of the day staff stayed until eleven to help, but then had to go. We had a late theatre list, so patients were still coming back to the ward at 10 pm.

One of these post ops was very ill and due to be transferred to another hospital first thing the next day for specialist treatment. She really needed to be in an intensive care unit.

At 1 am the silk dressing gown man buzzed, not for the first time, and I was the one who went to see what he needed.

'Can I have a tea tray, nurse? Earl Grey, please.'

'I'm really busy at the moment. I'll get it to you as soon as I can.'

That didn't happen, and at 2 am, he buzzed again. This time another nurse went. Same request, but not made as nicely this time. He got his tray, so, we thought, the end of the problem.

At 3 am he buzzed again. At this point we were trying desperately to keep our very ill patient alive, another patient had been violently sick because of his anaesthetic, and a third patient was in a lot of pain. Our resident doctor was going between them to try and keep all the plates spinning at once.

The senior nurse went into his room, cancelled the call button and sighed. 'Yes?'

'I asked for a tea tray at 1 am and 2 am,' he complained.

'Yes, and you got a tea tray at 2 I believe.'

'I asked for Earl Grey. That's not what I got. This isn't good enough.'

'I'm sorry, but we are busy.' With that she went out of his room, closing the door firmly as she left.

We didn't get breaks that night, and by morning all three of us felt dreadful. The first death had happened in this hospital, and that left us feeling defeated. Yes, people die even in private hospitals.

The nurse in charge went in to give the night report, but as she came out of the office the matron appeared and asked to speak to her. That man had complained about her. 'I want you to go into his room and apologise to him,' matron said.

'And if I don't?'

'Your position here will have to be reviewed.' It was in that moment that I saw the need to impress people in this hospital, both patients and their relatives. After all we had a reputation to keep up. This was a business at the end of the day.

The nurse was a single mum and needed this job, so she swallowed her pride and did as she was asked. In the changing room after, she was seething. 'He really enjoyed that. You should have seen the look on his face. Smug git!'

'He's going home today,' I soothed. 'We won't have to deal with him again.'

This was the one and only time I felt that management let us down at this hospital. Even though we had to tell other patients that we were too busy to get them a drink just when they wanted one, they were always understanding, and very grateful when we did manage to get them a drink. But I'll always remember the attitude of the silk dressing gown man — after all, he was a private patient.

Chapter 22

A right pain in the side!

Pain, they tell us, is subjective. For example, men are supposed to have a higher pain threshold than women, except apparently when it comes to childbirth. That's when we wonderful givers of life can stand excruciating agony to produce a tiny person. How and why we do this more than once can only be because of drugs, and/or nature playing a cruel trick on us females so we will keep the human race going! However, proving this theory can be very difficult.

We once had a wonderful scientific experiment on nights, in the shape of two males who had the same operation but reacted in a different way.

Patient number one was an athlete, a 24-year-old man. He was fit, healthy and came in for a planned appendectomy because he kept attending the local A&E department complaining of right lower quadrant abdominal pain.

He was always discharged without treatment and was given the diagnosis of 'grumbling appendix.' This, in itself is controversial. Some medical experts would say that there is no such thing. However, he was a top athlete at dominoes or some such thing, and these frequent bouts of pain were seriously impacting on his training schedule. He had seen one of our general surgeons in clinic who agreed to remove the troublemaker, put it in a specimen jar where it belonged and hey presto, problem solved.

Our second lab rat was one of those rarities, an emergency. A 14-year-old boy was seen by his GP at home and diagnosed with acute appendicitis needing immediate surgery. Mum had private medical insurance and worked on reception at our hospital, so after a few phone calls her son was on his way down to have his appendix removed by the same surgeon who had just finished operating on the athlete.

When we came on duty that night both patients were doing well post-op, pain relief had been given, and they were comfortable. I got the schoolboy to take care of, and one of my colleagues got the athlete as they were on different parts of the ward.

As I helped her to do the drugs round at about 10 pm we answered a buzzer from appendix number one, the athlete. He was in agony, rolling around the bed, holding his wound and crying in pain.

My first reaction was that something had gone wrong. 'I'll go and get Arthur,' (our in-house registrar). 'Go and get Arthur,' my colleague said at the same time, and it was obvious that she was thinking the same thing as I was.

Thirty minutes later, after another dose of pethidine, the athlete settled back to sleep.

'Not sure what's going on there,' said Arthur, scratching his head. He was as puzzled as we were.

All the patient's observations were normal apart from his BP being slightly raised. His wound was dry and clean and there was no indication of any issues from the surgery when his abdomen was examined. 'Keep an eye on him and give me a shout if you're concerned about him, though he should sleep for a week with all the opiates in his system.'

One of the last patients we saw on the drugs round, due to our slight delay, was the schoolboy, who was asleep. I did his observation while I was in his room and he opened one eye and looked slightly annoyed at being disturbed.

'How are you feeling?' I asked.

'Okay,' he said in a croaky voice.

'Any pain?'

'Not really.' With that, he closed his eyes and before I'd put out the light and instructed him to buzz if he needed anything, he was asleep.

A whole two hours went by before we heard from the athlete again. He buzzed and his nurse went to see what the issue was. She came swiftly back, bypassed our curious glances, and went straight to the doctor's room to get Arthur.

'What?' I asked as they both scurried past me. This must be serious, I thought, so I followed to see if I could help.

'I need another injection,' pleaded the athlete to Arthur as I got to the room. 'She said I can't have anything!' That last bit was spat out.

'Well, strictly speaking, the nurse is correct,' said Arthur. 'You've had more than you should have already. I can't understand why you're in pain so soon after your last injection.'

Everything was checked, and again, everything appeared normal. Arthur prescribed some codeine for the pain, and this seemed to work.

Arthur wrote all this up in the patient's notes. 'It was a straightforward removal. In fact, there were no signs of any inflammation of the appendix. He shouldn't be in so much pain.'

After this, I popped my head into the schoolboy's room. Still asleep. I did his observations and they were fine, and even though I was very quiet and gentle I disturbed him. It's difficult not to when someone is pulling back the bedclothes to make sure you're not bleeding to death, I suppose. But he was soon asleep again. He just wanted to be left alone.

The athlete managed to make it until the 6 am drug round before pleading for more analgesia.

He was given another injection but warned that he shouldn't need any stronger painkillers after this. He looked at us as if we had two heads. 'But I've had major surgery,' he protested.

'Not really,' said my colleague. 'You will only have a tiny scar, and you should be able to go home tomorrow.'

'I don't think so. I don't think I'll be in a fit state to go anywhere for, ooh, three to five days.'

We didn't say anything else and left him to his misery and pain.

When we got to the schoolboy, I was horrified to find him up. He was carefully making his way back to his bed after going to the toilet. 'You should have buzzed,' I said as I helped him.

Once back in bed, I asked if he had any pain. 'A bit,' he confessed.

'Would you like an injection?'

'No. I wouldn't mind a couple of paracetamols though.'

The irony of this was that we had to get Arthur up again, but this time to write up our little hero for simple paracetamol as he only had pethidine as an analgesic on his drug card.

I could easily say that the athlete was a wimp, in fact I did say that, come to think about it, but in truth, no one knows how they will react when they are in pain. Throughout my nursing career, I've seen so many people need extra-strong pain relief and others that do not need any when judging by their diagnosis and treatment, they should be in agony. We are all different, and we all handle what we go through in different ways, including physical pain.

Chapter 23

Who's who?

Most of the people walking through the doors of a private hospital, as I've already said, do so because they have a private insurance scheme which pays for all the care they need, from blood tests and consultation appointments to scans and actual operations. This can add up to a pretty penny, and before I left this establishment the managers had deemed that we night nurses didn't have enough to keep us busy, so they gave us the costing to occupy us in the wee small hours. This meant looking through the patient's records to see what care they had had, and putting a price on said care, even down to the tiniest of plasters.

Most of our patients were just ordinary people fortunate to have health insurance, but our customers would turn up in their best clothes, with new night attire and expensive toiletries. It was as if they had to prove they were entitled to be here, and act accordingly.

Then there was the man that broke the mould. A homeless man. I didn't really know if that were true or not, but when a patient turns up at 9 pm in a tatty suit which fitted where it touched, looking as if he hadn't had a haircut in years, and a case under his arm tied up with string, what was I supposed to think?

Mr. Smith was booked in, so he hadn't just chanced his luck to see if we had a spare bed he could spend the night in, but he was a conundrum to say the least.

I showed him to his room and offered to help him settle in. 'In what way?' he asked.

'Unpack. Get your PJ's on. And then admit you,' I replied.

'What does "being admitted" consist of, then?'

'Doing some paperwork. Checking your BP, pulse, temperature. Test your urine, all that sort of thing.'

'Well do what you must, then.' He wasn't unpleasant, just resigned. He also had a beautiful voice and I wondered how he had become homeless in the first place.

I did what I needed to do, but when I went to get his case so he could get ready for bed, he almost shouted at me to leave it where it was. 'I don't have night attire,' he informed me. 'Just provide me with some sort of gown and I'll sleep in that.'

I smiled, left him a pot to pee in, and said I'd be back later with the requested gown and take his water away. He had already refused a cup of tea, and was nil by mouth from midnight.

All the staff were busy doing the usual stuff when one of the consultant anaesthetists rocked up and asked for Mr. Smith's file. I gave it to him, and told him there was very little information in it. 'That's okay,' he said, with a smile. Unusual. This anaesthetist wasn't known for his good nature; that was why he had chosen this field to specialise in, as it meant he didn't have to talk to the patients much.

'Shall I accompany you?' I asked, getting ready to put down the water jug I was carrying, knowing he would expect me to go with him.

'No, that's fine, nurse. I'll see Mr. Smith on my own.' I almost dropped the jug as his reply caught me off guard and I missed the drinks trolley.

He reappeared about half an hour later and popped the file back into the trolley. It wasn't in the right place, but at least he tried.

We had, at last, sat down and were enjoying the first cup of tea of the night, speculating on our odd customer.

'I think he's some sort of government agent,' said one nurse.

'No, he's in a police protection scheme,' suggested another.

I was just about to put my thought on the subject to the panel when the door to the ward swung open with a clatter. That made us all jump, as once 11 pm came around, everywhere was locked up.

In strode one of our consultants. Of course, certain staff had access even when we were shut up for the night, in case of emergencies. 'Evening, girls. No, don't get up. Just point me in the direction of Mr. Smith's room.' Which we did.

He went into the room and closed the door firmly, but even so, we could hear jovial voices and laughter. Fifteen minutes later the surgeon came out, called a cheery farewell to the hobo, and left us in peace.

I duly went into the room at midnight to collect the jug and glass to prevent the man from having a drink. Each room had an en suite bathroom which meant that the person could go and get a drink if they really wanted to, but I suppose one might wake in the night and forget that they weren't supposed to consume anything before surgery, and by removing that temptation we were doing our best to enforce this rule.

I didn't see Mr. Smith again. He wasn't going to theatre until after lunch, so we left him to sleep in the next morning.

I was getting out of my uniform, when my colleague came into the changing room after giving the report to the day staff. 'Guess what I've just been told.'

'No, go on. I give up.'

'Mr. Smith!'

'What about Mr. Smith?'

'I know who he is.' She was stringing this out now.

'Look, I'm tired. I want to go home, have something to eat, hug my kids and then get some sleep.'

'He's a member of the royal family!' I wasn't expecting that, I must admit. 'And that case, it's got £15,000 in it, to pay for his stay.'

'What? In cash?'

She nodded. 'Doesn't trust banks, apparently.'

It transpired eventually that Mr. Smith was an Earl, or a Baron, or a Duke. We never really found out which, but he was stinking rich. That was partly because he didn't spend any money, and this could be seen by that state of his un-stately home which was falling down around his ears.

When he mentioned his 'pile' he meant it literally.

From royalty to bin men, we had them all. I became a patient in that hospital many, many years later, and I was treated like royalty. I was opposite a lady who was having the same op as me but under that NHS, and I did think that my utopian dream of everyone having this level of care had come true, even only in a small way.

PART FOUR
1999-2014

Chapter 24

Let's start again

Fast forward six years and you find me and mine in a new place, and in a new house because him indoors got a new job.

By this time I'd produced baby number four — the last one, I'd like to point out — and I was ready to look for a part-time job until the family was settled and I had found my feet.

Working in retail was the only job I'd done apart from nursing since starting a family, and this was where I found part-time employment once again.

I secured a position with a large department store and just did 16 hours each week, a full day on a Saturday, and another seven hours spread out between Monday and Friday. The money was rubbish, but the hours suited me, and I was working with a lovely team which made going in a pleasure.

I suspect I would have stayed there many more years if it hadn't been for my tardy line manager.

To be considered for promotion, and more importantly to get a pay rise, employees had to work through a task book. Each time you mastered a particular skill, your line manager signed it off in the book, and when the book was complete it went to HR. At this point you received a pay rise, and then went onto the next book. This was not complicated.

I had long filled my first book in and kept asking my manager if he had done his task, to which he would reply, 'This week.'

I was getting a little fed up with this response, but what did it for me was when a Saturday girl of about twelve (she was seventeen, she just looked twelve) asked if I would train her on till returns as she hadn't done that yet.

'No Problem. You need to get it signed off by a manager, though.'

'Oh, it already has been. I've had all my tasks signed off. In fact, I got a pay increase this week.'

I almost closed the till on her fingers.

I marched off to find my manager, and let him have it with both barrels. He apologised profusely, and promised to sort out his mistake by the end of next week.

But it was too little, too late. What with that little fiasco, and the fact that twelve months into this job I was doing more unsociable hours now than I would as a nurse, I decided to go back to my first career and see how that went. I applied for two jobs at the same time and got interviews for both in the same week.

The first one was working 20 hours a week at a geriatric (yep, there's that word again) hospital in another town. It was what I expected, and I decided I would take this job if I was offered it, and if the interview the following day didn't go well.

The second interview was for an EN post in the local day hospital. I had already phoned the sister and asked if I could go around the unit pre-interview, which I did. I immediately liked the set up, and took to the sisters who seemed very nice.

When I got a phone call from HR two days later it went something like this:

'Mrs Bissett?'

'Yes.'

'HR here, from the hospital.'

'Oh, yes?'

'You are in demand, aren't you?'

'Am I?'

'Yes. Not only have you been interviewed for two jobs with us, but you also been offered both positions.'

'Oh, good.'

'Good indeed. Now I'm presuming you're not wanting them both?'

'Oh, no, of course not.'

'So, which then?'

'The day hospital, please.'

'Jolly good. I'll let the other place down gently. Carry on like this and you'll be running the hospital in a few years.' With that she hung up, after telling me I would be hearing from them soon about police checks etc.

Four weeks later I began a 16-hour-a-week post in a familiar setting, and once again donned the uniform of a qualified nurse. I was a little apprehensive on my first shift as things tend to move rapidly in medicine. I worried I'd be out of touch, out of my depth and just look incompetent, which I probably did to some of the staff, since not all of them were as welcoming as the sister, but I think that was just because I was the new girl.

The job was much the same as it had been when I'd worked in the last day hospital, so it didn't take me too long to settle in.

One lady that came to us twice each week was having physiotherapy and seeing the occupational therapist and the dietician. Nora had suffered a severe stroke and was paralysed down one side. She also ate too much, partly because she was bored, and partly because she was depressed. Nora's GP gave her antidepressants which made her put even more weight on, and had a knock-on effect on her already greatly reduced mobility. We had to wave our magic wand and get her weight reduced and her mobility upgraded to adequate if not marvellous. The person suffering most, apart from Nora herself, was her son, who lived with her and was her carer.

Each time Nora came she would have intense physio, and we would weigh her once each week to see if she was complying with her diet. Sadly this seemed a lost cause, as her weight didn't alter much at all.

It came to a head the week her son brought her in saying that she had been having some 'funny turns', and could we investigate. Blood and urine tests proved that this lady had progressed to a type 2 diabetic.

The week after this diagnosis another discussion occurred with the dietician. 'Now, Nora, you need to stick to this diet like glue. Your blood sugars need to stay stable.' Nora nodded. 'Do you need me to phone your son and explain this?'

'No, I'll tell him all about it. Just give me that sheet of paper and he'll do the rest. He's a good boy.' This 'boy' was fifty-five if he was a day, and like his mother, he would just go with the flow, not taking anything on board that wasn't necessary.

The following week we weighed Nora, full of hope and expectations after she had sworn that she had stuck to the new diet as instructed. We were all gutted when we found she had put weight on, not lost it.

'Must be those new tablets that the doctor gave me,' she said by way of an excuse.

Week two of the new diet. More weight on, and the same the week after. At this point we called her son in for a case conference. That took place with all the agencies involved, most importantly the dietitian, who was concerned and confused by the lack of weight loss when Nora insisted that she was sticking strictly to her diet.

'I can't understand this. Does your mother manage to eat what's on the sheet?' she asked the son, who looked bored and slightly annoyed at having to take a few hours from work to attend. 'She does struggles to eat it all. It's too much.'

'Too much? In what way? If she isn't managing to eat what I suggested she should be losing weight, and quite a lot as well.'

'Well, she manages the food from the first diet sheet you gave her, but struggles to eat the stuff I make from the second one, you know, the one for her sugars.'

Every professional in the room looked at each other as the very large penny dropped.

'Both!' The poor dietician was flabbergasted. 'Not both! Just the latest one.'

'That's not what you told my mum, or at least, that's not what she told me.'

The moral of this story is that you can take a horse to water, but you can't make it drink. Nora carried on coming to us for another couple of months, and she did indeed lose some weight in that time, but I have a feeling that once discharged it all went back on again.

**

We often tested our patients to see if they were depressed or had the beginnings of dementia, both common in old age. These tests took the form of a series of questions, some of which I would have had trouble with even then. 'Count backwards from 100 in threes while balancing on your head. Name the prime minister of Kathmandu.' That sort of thing.

One lady was referred by her GP as he believed she was suffering from depression and possibly agoraphobia as well, as she was acting in a rather odd manner. Twice we sent for her, and twice she did not attend. Two strikes, and you're out. Consequently, we received yet another referral from her GP asking if we would send for her again, as she had recently become a widow and he was even more concerned about her mental health now.

We sent for her a third time, not thinking that we would see this lady, and blow me, she turned up the following week.

I'm not sure what I was expecting but it wasn't what was standing before me. I introduced myself and helped her off with her coat, showed her into the day room and sat her with some other patients who were having a cup of tea. She sat there chatting brightly with them and I took in her freshly permed hair, nice new clothes from M&S, and just a touch of makeup. She didn't look depressed to me, but people, as I had learned over the years, are very good at hiding things.

The cup of tea over, we moved into the doctor's room to have a chat. I did her observations and took her through the tests for mental health and forgetfulness. She came out at the other end with her results within a normal range, whatever that is these days.

'Now, Agnes, how do you feel in yourself?'

'Fine, ducks.'

'Yes, but you must be sad. I see you recently lost your husband?'

'That's why I'm fine now. He was a cruel bastard, and he made my life a misery. I danced around his grave, literally. I waited until everyone had left the graveside and then did a little jig.'

'But your GP was concerned because he thought you were depressed!'

'I was depressed. Living with him made me depressed.'

'Right. So, you're not depressed?'

'Never felt better. Especially now I get to spend his money, and mine. He would get my old age pension every month and I never saw a penny of it. He just put it in a case under the bed.

Thousands of pounds were squirrelled away there. And now I'm going to spend, spend, spend.' She said this with a massive smile on her face.

Later our doctor sent her for some routine blood tests, and we told her we would see her next week for the results.

'Sorry, I can't come next week; I'm going on a cruise with my friend Ethel.'

'All right, when you return, then,' I said.

She winked. 'Fine, I'll see you in six months!'

In report, after they had all departed, I told the rest of the team her story. 'She was married to him for 45 years and he treated her like dirt. Why didn't she just leave?'

'Wasn't so easy then,' a colleague replied. 'You were ostracized if you were a divorced woman, and she probably wouldn't have had any money of her own.'

All I could add to that was 'Bon voyage, Agnes!'

Chapter 25

I have the power!

We changed sisters' mid-way through my time on the day hospital. The outgoing sister, who was now a friend, decided to retire. A newer younger model was put in her place, and encouraged me to apply for the conversion course to take me to first-level registration.

In theory any EN still working in the NHS should have been given this opportunity, though some were quite happy with their lot and declined this offer. I thought about it and what it would mean for my career, and decided to have a go.

It was two years of self-study, with days in the nursing school once a month. We also had to visit disciplines we had never had a chance to work on and write essays. At the end of the course we had to submit a 5000-word dissertation.

There were about twelve of us and some were keener than others, but I did realise very early on in the course that we were being trained to be managers. I suppose that's all they could give us extra training for in reality, as EN did almost every job a RN would do by this point in time.

Overall, I think the group enjoyed the course and we supported each other when feeling overwhelmed.

I chose to do some community experiences outside of the hospital, and work on the maternity unit to increase my practical skills, and boy did that open my eyes.

Ambulance:

I spent one twelve-hour shift with an ambulance crew and the first call we went to at 7 am was that of a young woman who was pregnant and a diabetic. She lived with her mum and was having problems with her insulin. She kept having hypoglycemic episodes and had phoned both her GP and midwife for advice. 'Get yourself to the hospital,' they recommended, so she found us on her doorstep to take her there.

She was so scared, as was her mum, but when we got to the hospital there was no room on the maternity ward, so we were told to take her up the gynae ward just for the morning. They reassured her that they would have a bed by lunchtime that day.

As we walked onto the gynae ward, an auxiliary greeted us with 'Oh great. That's just what we need!' To say she was less than pleased to see us was an understatement. The patient started to cry, and her mum looked as if she was about to explode.

I was furious and took this nurse to one side. 'Excuse me, but that poor girl is frightened enough without that sort of greeting.' The auxiliary apologised, saying they had had the night from hell, and she was at the end of her tether. 'You had better explain that to them,' I replied. I don't know if she did, as we had to leave to go to another emergency, but I was ashamed to be a nurse at that moment.

The case we were called to was that of a man with chest pains. His GP was with him and wanted him transported to A&E post haste — remember the good old days when GP's still came out to see you when you were ill? I was slightly nervous in case he died on us en route, but when we got there he didn't look as bad as I thought he should if he was having a heart attack.

As the hospital was only a five minute drive away we didn't attach any cables or put any sharp things near this patient; we just put on blues and twos and got on our way. The thrill of the noise, the parting of the traffic, the speed of the vehicle — this was great!

I accompanied the gentleman into A&E with the paramedics and once again I was met with slight hostility. 'Sorry, you can't go in there,' said a senior nurse in blue with an attitude, 'there' being resus, 'go and give your husband's details to the front desk and we will come and get you when the doctor's done the assessment.'

My coat, over my uniform, was causing the issue, and so I flashed my uniform at the human wall that was stopping me from learning! Her attitude changed completely, and I was waved through to the resuscitation room with the patient and the ambulance crew. However, once again my hackles were up.

If I had been that man's wife, I'm not sure I would have been happy with the way I was spoken to. You come into this department usually vulnerable and afraid and what you don't want is some jobsworth telling you to go away.

We handed the patient over to the medics, went back to the ambulance station and had a slow, quiet afternoon, where I watched a great deal of TV.

My shift was almost over when we got a call to the local bowling alley. A female had fallen and hurt her back, so off we trotted again.

The lady in question was lying halfway up one of the alleys in a great deal of discomfort, made worse by the fact that about fifty people had a full view of her predicament.

I and one of the paramedics walked gingerly on the very slippery surface to assess the damage. 'How on earth did your mange this?' asked the paramedic, with a smile on his face.

'I forgot to let go of the ball,' she said. We tried not to laugh; after all, we were professionals, and this woman was in pain.

The paramedic with me instructed his colleague to bring gas and air, a scoop and a neck brace.

In the meantime we did a quick general assessment, and it was both our opinions that no serious damage had been done. 'However,' said the man in green, 'we are going for belt and braces here, so don't be concerned about all the paraphernalia we're going to use. Better safe than sorry.'

Paramedic number 2 was soon back and I went to help him with the equipment. We looked like Bambi on ice, slipping and sliding and juggling equipment. It must have been hilarious for the crowd.

The woman used the gas and air as if her life depended on it, and with that we managed to get her neck brace on, scooped her onto a metal stretcher, and were ready for our onward journey.

Once we were underway we tried to take the gas and air from her as she had relaxed a bit too much, but that wasn't going to happen any time soon! 'This stuff is fucking good,' she said, and started giggling. We decided to leave it with her and giggled along.

I enjoyed my shift with the ambulance service and even though we did sit around a lot, it was exciting when we were on 'a shout'. I don't think the service today resembles the service I went out with. No long boring sessions back at the station. Now GPs don't do house visits unless you are dying or bedridden, and never out of hours. With cutbacks, a rising number of people suffering from mental health issues, and drug and alcohol misuse, these wonderful people still turn up day after day and look after us. They are FABULOUS!

I never did find out what happened to the patients I dealt with that day, which is often the case for the paramedics who get patients to A&E alive. I have to say that my son and myself attended the same A&E years later as patients, and we had the best care possible. Maybe I just caught one person on an off day, and we all have them now and again.

District midwife:

Everyone who was a trained midwife wanted this job. They had the sole responsibility for running clinics at GP surgeries, delivering babies both in people's homes and in hospital, doing home visits after delivery to check mother and baby, then handing the whole lot over to the health visitor after ten days. Job's a good 'un!

Even I fancied the idea, except for the problem that no one ever seemed to leave, and you had to wait until someone retired before a vacancy came up. As I was in my forties at this point I didn't think I would be in the running for the next post, even if I did the midwifery training and got a few years of experience in a hospital setting under my belt. But it was a nice thought.

I went to a GP clinic with my allocated midwife and she asked each patient if they minded me being there. Not one mum-to-be said yes, and it was a great morning watching them have their antenatal checks, asking questions, getting advice, and looking happy about their little bumps.

The last patient we saw didn't have the same glow about her as the others. She looked about fourteen, but her card told me she was eighteen years old, this was her first baby, and she was 28

weeks pregnant. She had dark circles under her eyes, and seemed sort of defeated. After the midwife had examined her, she sat down and filled in various forms.

Now for the Q&A, I thought, and I wasn't wrong.

What I was wrong about was the advice this young lady was going to receive from her lovely midwife.

'So, how is it going?' The midwife said matter-of-factly.

'Okay, I suppose.'

'Still smoking?'

'Yeah. But just cigs, not pot any more. Well not often, anyhow.' She looked down at her hands.

'But you've given the coke up?'

'Oh, yeah.' A shrug of the shoulders.

'Drinking?'

'Yeah.'

'How much?'

'A couple of glasses a day.'

'Good.' With that the midwife closed her book in which she had been taking notes and smiled at the young mum-to-be. Good? Was this midwife mad? Didn't she have the right to get this pregnant teenager taken into care? Couldn't we stop her abusing her body, and her baby?

'Well done, you're doing great. Just try and knock the wine on the head. Will you do that?'

'I'll try.' With that she picked up her card and went, leaving me with an astonished look on my face. I couldn't quite believe I had just been privy to that conversation.

'You look shocked,' the midwife said with a slight smile.

'I am. Doesn't she realise the harm she is doing to that baby?'

'She does.'

'And?'

'And at the moment she doesn't care. But I'm making progress.'

'Won't the baby be damaged?'

'Possibly.'

'Possibly?'

She looked at me. 'Probably, but we will deal with that then.'

'Why is she having a baby at all?'

'Life is complicated. She didn't even know she was pregnant until a few weeks ago. She has come a long way in a short time, and I don't want to put her under too much pressure. I want her to trust me and keep attending her antenatal appointments.'

'You see all sorts, don't you?'

'Just wait for this next one. Come on, we have a home visit to do.'

It was an ordinary house on an ordinary street. 'We are going to see a lass who is 24 weeks pregnant and make sure her home is suitable to bring a baby back to after delivery.'

'And what if it isn't?'

'Then we plan an intervention. Get social services involved, look at alternative accommodation. In this case I know the home setting is good, but we do this sort of visit as routine these days.'

As we parked the midwife spoke again. 'It's not just the domestic circumstances that we are looking at today.'

'Why? What do you mean?'

'You'll see.' Mysterious.

A young girl answered the door and shyly let us in. 'Hi, how are you today?' the midwife said after introducing me. The girl just nodded and invited us into the sitting room, which was modern and clean. Lots of cream. Cream carpets, furniture and décor, with the odd dot of silver here and there. Not to my taste, but very nice. We all sat down, and the midwife chatted as she did the girl's blood pressure and then got her to lie on the settee while she felt her bump and listened to the baby's heartbeat.

'All good. You're doing well. How are mum and dad these days? Getting used to things?'

'Slowly,' she said, looking down. 'It's not easy for them.'

'You're still their little girl,' said the midwife kindly.

'What about John? Will they let him visit you here, or do you still have to meet on neutral ground?'

'He can come here if they're here, but they won't speak to him.'

'Give them time.'

'Well, I'm sixteen in six weeks so they won't be able to stop us then. We are going to live together, and that's all there is to it.'

'I'm sure once they see their grandchild and get used to the fact that you're a mum it will be easier.'

We made our way back to the midwives' office, and I asked what the issues were surrounding the young girl's pregnancy.

'Her partner, the father of the baby, is — sorry, was — her father's best friend. He's forty and she is fifteen, so as you might imagine, they are not wild about the circumstances.'

If I thought the case before this had been outside my comfort zone, this was in a different country. 'But isn't that abuse, I mean rape? Why hasn't he been arrested? Surely he's a ...' I searched for the word.

'Paedophile?'

'Yes.'

'As far as the law is concerned, yes, he is, but he has never done anything like this before. I've seen them together and they do seem truly in love. He is so excited about the baby and he does want to marry her.'

'So, no police?'

'No police.'

I was stunned, but the girl had threatened to run away if her parents went to the police. She also said she would claim she became pregnant after a one-night stand and didn't know who the father was. Hence it was not reported.

It was a doomed relationship as far as I could see, but I hoped I was wrong.

Maternity ward:

I did three days on the maternity unit, which was very quiet when I was there. I didn't see a normal delivery, which I was hoping for, but having had four children myself I had a good idea of what went on. I was, however, privileged to see a Caesarean section, which was amazing.

All gowned up I went to talk to the mum, as there seemed to be a lot of people around the business part of her abdomen. I held her hand on one side of the operating table, and her husband held her hand on the other side.

After a lot of tugging and pulling a very loud healthy baby was held up for mum and dad to see, and then taken to the paediatrician for a quick check. I was crying, dad was crying, and mum was just holding our hands to make sure we were both all right, more worried about us than we had a right to.

That was so joyful, but I also saw the other side of the coin, so to speak. I was shadowing one of the sisters on the maternity ward when she received a phone call asking her to see a couple coming in from the clinic, because the mum-to-be needed an urgent scan.

When they arrived they were both ashen. The technician, a doctor, and the sister all went into the side ward with the couple. I followed them, but I was told to stay out, which I was indignant about. How could I learn if I was excluded? I sat down to wait and read some case notes to pass the time.

The technician came out first and the doctor not long after, but the sister was in there for ages. When she finally emerged from the room, she went off to make up a tea tray, which she took back into the side ward.

Sister looked distracted when she finally got back to me, and I felt I should offer to make her some hot sweet tea. 'Are you okay?' I asked.

'Not really. I'll never get used to that.'

'To what?'

'Their baby has died in the womb, but she will have to go through labour anyway.'

'Oh.' That was all I could muster.

'Oh, indeed. That's why I didn't want you in the room. They had enough people in there, they didn't need an onlooker as well.'

I got it. It isn't always about me. Regardless of the fact students are there to learn, sometimes it just isn't right to be included in the most tragic and private moments.

Special baby unit:

I just had one day here. Again, they were quiet, and only had two babies in needing specialist treatment.

The first baby was a prem. He had been born four weeks early with a low birth weight, even considering his early arrival into this world. He had tubes going in and out of all sorts of places. It all looked very scary, so goodness knows how his mum and dad felt. They hovered around his cot dressed in the white gowns that did their best to protect these tiny humans from all our grown-up bugs and bacteria. The doctors felt confident that he would be home with his parents once he had put on a little weight, and could maintain his body temperature.

The other baby was having withdrawal symptoms from his mother's heroin addiction. This tiny scrap was being given drugs regularly to try and stop the convulsions and the awful screaming which were just a few of the terrors this child was going through.

I discussed his prognosis with one of the doctors on the unit. 'He may be brain damaged, we just don't know yet,' he told me. 'I expect he'll be with us for a while and then he'll be transferred to a children's hospital for ongoing treatment.'

It just seemed so sad. Yesterday I'd been told about a loving couple who had lost their much-wanted child, and today a baby would, in all probability, be taken into care by social services because his mum couldn't care for him. But then, who said life was fair?

Chapter 26

Not the end, just the beginning

Our course was almost over. We had to submit our 5000-word study, which was to be marked, and the adjudicators had to make sure we had accrued all the hours we needed on other specialties. Then we would find out if we had cut the mustard.

At the beginning of the course I had said I wanted to stay on at the day hospital; I didn't have any reason to move on, pass or fail, and I was more than happy with my lot. Of course, things had changed. I had tasted the food of possibilities, drunk at the fountain of future dreams, and now wanted more — if I passed of course.

Staying would mean that things had stayed the same. I might, if I were lucky, get a small wage increase, and I could wear a different colour belt, but that was all. If I applied for other jobs that required a first level registration, it opened up a whole new world for me.

Then everything was thrown into sharp focus, and all those considerations suddenly didn't matter.

I was at work. It was the day before I got my final marks; Tuesday the 11th of September, 2001. We were serving lunch to the patients when a physiotherapist ran into the day room, went straight to the TV, and switched it on without so much as a by your leave.

'What do you think you're doing?' said our auxiliary, with her hands on her hips and a frown on her face.

He didn't say anything, and he didn't need to as the pictures of the Twin Towers in New York became clear on the screen.

'What's going on? Is that skyscraper on fire?' I asked as the whole room became quiet. No one got a chance to voice an opinion as just then the second jet hit the second tower, live on air. We were witnessing a terrorist attack like no other in history.

We watched events unfold. Even though they were horrifying and upsetting, we couldn't tear our eyes away from the screen, finding it hard to believe what we were seeing. What would this mean? How many people had died? Who had carried out this atrocious act? So many questions, so much fear and so much sadness.

I went home that evening and watched the whole thing again, and then again, finding out about the Pentagon being a target, about one aircraft that crashed. It was like some terrible nightmare.

I don't think I slept much that night, and I suspect I wasn't the only one, and the next day seemed not to matter in the least.

Our group met in one of the classrooms at the hospital education center, and of course our conversations were not about our final course marks, but of the previous day's events. We were meeting our tutor here, and she was giving us back our studies, together with our marks. Some of us would have to present our case studies as well, but we didn't know who, and we were told we all had to be prepared to do this if called upon.

Our tutor was an easy-going woman, and we all liked her. She got the best from us and tried to make the work interesting and, when possible, fun.

'She's late,' commented one of our number, checking her watch. She was indeed late, which was unusual, but not long after this comment she appeared.

'Right, let's go into a smaller room. This one is needed.' We followed her and asked her what she thought of the events of the last 24 hours. 'We are here to talk about you,' she said, 'this is your day.' She looked tired and pale, and not quite herself. 'I have great pleasure in telling you all that you have passed!' A quiet scream went up, plus a few hugs and kisses. We were handed back our work and I saw that I got through by the skin of my teeth, but did I care? Not at all.

The work was gone through and then I was asked to present my study. Taken aback, I did my best and talked through the work I had done on an enhanced type of stress test that was carried out in my department. It was okay as these girls were now my friends, and it wasn't a task to talk to them.

When I finished, we saw our tutor smile. 'Well done, all of you.'

'Are you all right?' someone asked.

'Yes. I need to go, though. I've got things to do. Congratulations, ladies.' And with that, she was gone.

'Not herself, is she?' someone remarked.

Over the following weeks we learned more of what had happened on 9/11, as the terrible details started to emerge. Over three thousand people died that day, and one of that number was the brother of our tutor.

Chapter 27

The grass is always greener

I did indeed move on. I applied for and got a job as a practice nurse for a group of GPs in a local town, about two years after I completed my conversion course. During this time I had also done a mentorship course. I didn't want to, but I was to find that no education is ever wasted, and thanked my then manager, yet again, for nagging me to do it.

I thought that this job would be a pushover. I thought I would be able to do it standing on my head. I thought wrong. I struggled a great deal with some of the work; the criteria that had to be reached, the blood test results that meant nothing in one patient's medical history, but something in another's, and just when I was starting to get a grip on the system, didn't all the GPs go and renegotiate their contracts with the GMC! This turned the whole system on its head. GPs had to look upon their practices as a business, and because of this some doctors left, saying that they wanted to help sick people, not their bank balance.

For me, it meant I got moved to the treatment room. This was an area that in the past had been treated like a very minor A&E, where we took out sutures, changed dressings, gave injections, took blood, did ear syringing, family planning and minor surgery, to name but a few.

Now I found myself wondering why I was doing a job I hadn't even applied for. I was not happy.

'Don't worry,' they said, 'we will give you the necessary training.'

'Don't worry,' they said, 'we will support you.' They didn't do either.

I tried; Lord knows I tried. I went to management again and again to ask for help, but the only thing I got was a few more hours each week so that I could see more patients. The more people we saw, the more points the GPs got. And what do points make? Yes, you've guessed it, prizes.

The final straw was the day I was asked to do a dressing on a young man who had presented at A&E the day before with a deep cut to his leg. Strictly speaking he should have gone back to the hospital for this under the new rules, as the GPs wouldn't get paid for this service any longer. However, there was a mix up in communications and I ended up with the task.

The man in question was pleasant enough, if not a little strange. He had a slightly haunted look about him. I was halfway through the procedure when one of the GPs rushed into the room. 'Okay, Carol?' he asked, slightly breathless.

'Yes.' Strange, I thought.

'You okay, Rob?' he asked the patient, he obviously was familiar with this patient.

'Fine, doc. Well, not fine, otherwise I wouldn't be here, would I?'

The GP nodded and started looking through some notes while whistling quietly to himself. I finished the dressing, told the patient he now needed to go to a dressing clinic at the general hospital to have his stitches out, and waved him goodbye.

The GP looked very relieved. 'Glad he's gone. Though he was as good as gold today, wasn't he?'

'Why wouldn't he be?' I asked absentmindedly as I cleared up the dressing trolley. He might have time to stand and chat, but I certainly didn't. I was, as usual, running late, which meant more unpaid overtime. This, I was assured, I could take as holidays, just as soon as things got quiet.

'Well, with his police record, plus the drugs ... and that knife wound. Had the security blokes pulling him off a doctor in A&E yesterday. He can be a bit unpredictable.'

I stood looking at this man with disbelief on my face. 'Was I in danger?'

'I came in, didn't I?'

I wasn't sure if he wanted a medal or my undying gratitude, but he got neither. 'That's it. I'm out of here. I don't get paid enough or treated well enough to risk life and limb.'

'I think you're a bit over the top there,' he said, with a smile on his face. That was the wrong thing to say.

The next day I handed in my notice and was told by the practice manager that the partners wouldn't react well to a threat. I carefully and slowly placed the envelope in front of her, smoothing down the corners before I let it go. 'It's not a threat,' I said, in a very quiet voice. 'It's a promise.'

Not one GP came to see me after I had given them my resignation to try and talk me round, and on my last day I got a pathetic bunch of flowers as an afterthought. The practice manager took my lead and left shortly after had saying, 'Life's too short'. And did I get my hours back that I had worked without pay? Of course not!

The one thing that I did get from my time as a practice nurse was immunisation training. This was so that I could do childhood and flu vaccinations, and the course was free to my employers.

When I went for my interview at the practice I was promised the earth where training was concerned, all of which I was eager to do, and I never saw any of it, except this course.

'How do you feel about vaccinating children and adults?' they asked.

'Fine,' I lied. The thought of sticking sharp needles into small cubby limbs just made me shiver with horror. 'Good. We'll sort you out some training as soon as possible.'

I managed to avoid this for a few months. 'Oh, imms and vaccs training. When? I'm away that week. what a shame.' Or 'Imms and vaccs training. Wouldn't you know it, I've got a full clinic that day, and no one to cover for me.' Cue sad face.

Eventually the practice manager came into my office one day. 'You're on the imms and vaccs training the week after next. And before you protest, I've rearranged your clinic, checked you're not on holiday, and there isn't a full moon.'

I looked at her, confused. 'Full moon?'

'Well, you've used every other excuse in the book.' Then she went before I had time for any sort of remark.

The imms training was in the morning, and the afternoon was dedicated to something called 'anaphylactic shock,' which I had heard of, but not in the detail we immunisers needed to know about the subject. I think by the end of the day I was suffering from some sort of shock. I couldn't believe that we were now expected to go and stab children and adults with all these chemicals, and I hadn't got a clue what they did or if they were dangerous.

I shadowed a health visitor who was doing an immunisation clinic for a few weeks, and then flew solo, still not confident about what I was doing. The actual procedure of giving an injection wasn't the issue here; it was the information around it plus the science of the vaccines. What are they made of? What side effects can they have? When shouldn't you give them? What happens if you give the wrong injection? What happens if they drop dead?

I was having sleepless nights and dreaded the clinics I had to do, even though they were simple and I had good paperwork to guide me, plus a clerical assistant who did all the computer input.

Then one day a medical rep asked if she could see me. She had heard on the grapevine that I was now doing immunisations and was touting her wares, which happened to be travel vaccines. 'I don't do them,' I declared, and shivered at the prospect of yet another nightmare on the horizon. 'I'm struggling with the childhood vaccines, let alone the complicated issues of travel vaccines.' The rep had sat down, and unfortunately for her I was in a mood to unload. She didn't look bored at all, but after about forty-five minutes she did look at her watch. 'I think we might be able to help, if you would like that.'

'Can you do the clinics for me?' I asked hopefully.

She laughed the laugh of the free and easy. 'No, but I could investigate some training courses and perhaps my company could give you some money towards it? And maybe the practice could top that up.'

When I had stopped giggling, I said there was no chance of that, but I would be very interested and grateful for anything they could suggest or help me with.

Two days later I received an email from her telling me about a three-day course in Manchester, and an offer of half the fees, which was very reasonable in my opinion. I made my mind up that I would put the shortfall in, as it would be worth every penny. But adding travel expenses, accommodation and food to that would make it more than I could reasonably afford. The course was a few months hence. I booked my slot and hoped that the rest would work out, which it did.

Before the course started, I had taken my leave from the GP practice and started a short-term contract with the Health Visiting service as an HV assistant. We dealt with the elderly and did visits to check their medication, how they were, follow up on any A&E attendance and tried to refer them on to other agencies when necessary. I also assisted one of my colleagues with an immunisation clinic, which she did on behalf of the trust for the GP's.

She also felt that she needed more information about this part of her role, but she came across as very confident, and the mums, dads and children trusted her. Then she went off on long term sick leave, and guess which mug they got to fill in — yes, this mug!

When my manager approached me I was hesitant, but she wasn't telling me I had to do it, she was asking me. 'I'm on a course in two weeks,' I told her. 'Maybe when I've done that?'

She looked at her computer and clicked a few buttons. 'What course? We haven't booked you onto any courses so far.'

'No, I booked myself onto this course before I left the practice, and I'm self-funding and taking holidays,' I finished, before she could object.

'Oh, right. Well done. Tell you what, I'll do the next few clinics with you, I'll try and get you some finance towards your expenses, and you can have those days as study leave if you will take over the imms clinics.'

'What, until Pam gets back from her sick leave?'

'No, permanently. I get the feeling Pam won't want to go back to the imms clinics.' She was good. She had smooth-talked me into a corner and I had no way out.

'Okay,' I said, wondering if I was going to live to regret this little compromise.

Chapter 28

Best job ever?

'Do you realise how many lives you save each year by doing this job? And it's a thankless task; stabbing tiny babies, crying toddlers, and pre-schoolers that bite back. But you are amazing. You are the public health force that doesn't get the recognition they deserve. You are heroes.'

Quite an introduction I thought, but straight away this man had us in the palm of his hand. He made us feel special; his enthusiasm was as infectious as the diseases we were fighting.

Doctor Baxter, immunisation supremo. I was to come across him many times in the future, but this was his course. It was nationally known, and I was on it.

Day one was the immune system. But I had done my research; well, I'd borrowed a 'basic' book on the immune system from my scientific daughter. 'It's easy reading, Mum,' she said as she handed it over to me. I was glad that my course didn't require me to board an aircraft as that book would seriously dent my luggage allowance. I had the book, and I even tried to read the first few chapters, but after a page or two, I wondered why it was written in a different language; that of the geek.

When our course leader started talking about type B lymphocytes, T helper cells and macrophages, all I could see was flying saucers, which most of them looked like. I did hope this course was going to get easier, or at least that they were going to use words I could understand.

During the first break I was getting a much-needed coffee to take my paracetamol with, as my brain was starting to hurt, when a voice behind me said, 'Why, if it isn't Mrs Bissett.' I turned to see a colleague from the HPA, (Health Protection Agency) whom I had met only once, in passing. 'Good course to be on. Are you enjoying it so far?'

'I'm trying to understand it, that would do.'

She laughed. 'Me too.' Then she took her drink and went back to sit with her colleague. By the end of the day I realised I was among doctors, consultants, senior practice nurses and trainers. I was beginning to think I was out of my league, but I was here now and going to make the best of it.

Day two was about vaccines, their constituents and side effects. This I lapped up, making copious notes and hanging on every word. After I had dinner that evening at my 2-star hotel, I went to my room, phoned home and then studied.

Day three was just the icing on the cake — all the myth and disinformation that surrounds vaccines and what they do to the body. This was the most interesting and useful part of the course as far as I was concerned.

When it finished and I was driving home I reflected on how I felt before the course and how I felt now. More confident, yes; more informed, definitely. I was all fired up to take on that weekly clinic and I was going to do it well. No, more than that — I was going to do it and feel that I was part of the public health team who stop people dying from diseases which have, in the past, killed thousands.

Chapter 29

And then there was one

I'm not quite sure how it happened, but within eight months of completing this excellent course I was doing 25 immunisations clinics each month, in and around the area. This was all I did now and I was getting all the practice I needed, as well as a reputation with the practice staff and parents.

We provided the service for GPs, who were paid to do the dirty deed, but didn't see the need since it had historically been done by the health visiting service. Like the health visitors, I worked for the community health trust. This gave me a say in how things ran; not much, but it was better than nothing.

I also had a temporary contract which had been renewed twice already, and I was warned by my manager that it was looking less and less probable that they would have the money to renew it a third time.

However, once again fate took me in her gracious hands and helped me out. I had arranged to have some holidays, not unreasonable in this day and age. I filled in the necessary forms, notified the necessary people, and went off for a family break.

When I came back, there were complaints from parents, and some from GPs, at almost every clinic I took. No one had been available to fill in for me, so while I was away most of the appointments were cancelled, some at very short notice, as in, when people turned up with their child under one arm, and their appointment letter under the other. I got it in the neck from somebody at every venue and was getting slightly fed up of taking the flak for someone's mismanagement. 'This just isn't good enough,' one dad said in an angry voice.

'I agree,' I said as I checked his documentation.

'I took time off work to come with my wife, only to get here and be told the clinic had been cancelled because there was no one to do it.' He glared at me.

'That's correct.' I couldn't argue with the man, he was right.

'It's just not good enough.'

'I know.'

'I'm going to complain.'

'Please do.'

'What?'

'Please complain. I'll get you the detail of where to send your complaint to.'

'Oh. All right.' I don't know what he was expecting as a response, but it wasn't the one he had received from me. As the man left the receptionist smiled. 'That took the wind out of his sails.'

'What do you mean?' I asked, as I tidied up my equipment.

'Calling his bluff like that. They never do complain you know, so don't worry.'

'I'm actually hoping he does. Nothing is going to change if no one points out the problems in the system. The powers that be certainly won't listen to me.' That took the wind out of her sails as well.

With unemployment looming, I had applied for a post as a school nurse and been called for an interview, and then I got a phone call from my manager. 'Carol, the chief exec got a complaint about the slack in the imms service from a dad that attended one of your clinics.'

'Oh, so he did complain then. Good!'

'Yes, definitely good, because I told her your temporary contract was finished and you were looking at other posts.'

'Right?'

'She told me to offer you a permanent contract post-haste before we lost you.'

I was thrown by this having got use to the idea that my contract would soon be coming to an end.

'Interesting.'

'What do you think?'

'I need to think about it. I've got this interview, and I'd sort of made my mind up that if they offer it to me, I'll take it. After all, the school nurses have to do vaccinations as well.'

'Yes, of course. But there would be four extra hours a week on offer so that you can work with the TB (Tuberculosis, a bacterial infection, usually of the lungs) specialist nurse.'

'I'll take it.'

Okay, I'm weak, but inside I was very happy.

Chapter 30

A plum job

The TB specialist nurse was a treasure. She taught me a great deal and we became friends very quickly. I was fascinated by the subject, TB in general and the disease in England in particular.

I joined the service around the time that the BCG ceased being given in secondary school as a matter of course; four little pricks and a jab, as it was known locally. This caused a bit of an outcry, and I was to see later in my immunisation career that there was always a protest of some sort when we introduced a new vaccine into the immunisation program, and when we withdrew one. You can't win, really.

The withdrawal put more pressure on the service to start with, because there was still the need in some instances for the BCG to be given, so referrals came at us thick and fast.

I was trained to do the Mantoux test (the four little pricks) as well as BCG vaccinations. I watched my mentor as she skillfully performed this difficult vaccination, and then went and practised on a plum at home with the correct syringe and water, thus allowing said fruit to be stewed once I'd finished practicing my skills on it. After a while I had it perfected but was soon to find that while plums don't move when you approach with a sharp instrument, humans do.

The BCG wasn't just a straight-in straight-out type of vaccination. The recipient had to hold very still while a fine needle was inserted just under the skin on the upper arm and the fluid was gently pushed in to form a blob. Because it was going just under the skin the needle didn't really hurt, but the vaccine did.

The WHO (World Health Organization) decided that mass TB vaccination were not needed in all countries, including the UK as our rates of TB cases were thankfully low, apart from some clusters in inner cities.

One job that was more important, because of the new rules, was assessing immigrants coming into the UK from countries that still had this killer disease at epidemic proportions. I saw a lady from Russia one day who was under the impression that I could help with her visa application. Once I had put her straight on that subject we got chatting, and she told me she had been a nurse in a remote area of her homeland.

'Ve ad a doctor vonce a week in good weather,' she said, in broken English which was better than my Russian, 'and vonce a month in bad climate.'

'Once a month!' Oh how spoilt we are in this country.

'If ve ver lucky.'

'How did you manage?'

She shrugged. 'Ve made best of vat we had.'

'What was that?'

'Wodka.'

'Wodka? Oh, vodka!' I nodded. This was a drink which held many medicinal properties.

'What I said, wodka.'

'But what about influenza?'

'Wodka and lemon.'

"Wounds?'

'Straight wodka.'

'Sterilizing equipment?'

'Industrial wodka. Sort that makes you blind if you drink it.'
I'll never complain about the NHS again.

Chapter 31

Taking the rough with the smooth

I covered a big area during my years as an immunisation nurse and saw a vast difference in the type of people I dealt with. They ranged from the middle class in one town to working-class/unemployed in another, but they were just people to me. However, one day the difference in attitude towards how the two class groups viewed my speciality came into sharp focus.

I spent the morning in a very middle-class area where money wasn't an issue in general, and unemployment was low. I had just one more pre-school booster to give before I had lunch and went to the next town to do more clinics.

We called in our last customer and along came four-year-old Sebastian with his mum trailing behind him. My heart sank as the child in question entered the room wearing a thick quilted coat, gloves and a hat. It was July and a toasty 18 degrees outside. My concerns were further compounded when Sebastián shot under my desk and grabbed one of its legs, holding on for dear life. This, I thought, isn't going to be easy.

I ignored the child while I introduced myself and my colleague to his mother. My clerical assistant was there to do the paper-work for me but did so much more, sweet talking the parents and children, holding babies for me as mothers ran out of the room crying, and getting me endless cups of tea.

I checked we had the right child, that he was having the right vaccinations, that he was well (if somewhat hot), and what age he was. I explained which diseases the vaccines we were giving would prevent, and what mum should look for in the way of side effects. 'Right, so if you just get Sebastian ready, I'll draw up the vaccines,' I concluded hopefully.

Mum pushed her chair back and tried to take hold of her son's arm. 'Come on out, Seb, there's a good boy.'

'NO!'

'Now, Seb. We talked about this over dinner last night, didn't we? And you said you would be brave.'

'NO!'

'Now, Sebastian, mummy is going to get vexed. No cakes for you if you don't come out.'

'Don't want any!'

At last she reached under the table and dragged her uncoop-erative child from his hiding place.

As she tried to take his coat off he put it back on again. One arm out, one arm in. It was like doing the hokey cokey. Even with our friendly help things we were getting nowhere fast and Sebastian was getting more and more agitated, to the point where he was screaming blue murder, kicking, and trying to bite anything that came near his mouth.

I gave up. 'I'm sorry, but this isn't going to work. Take him home and I'll recall him in a couple of weeks.'

'Oh. Well if you think that's best.' I'm not sure if his mum was annoyed with me or relieved. 'His father will have to bring him next time. I can't go through this again.'

'Good. But can I suggest that you put a short-sleeved T-shirt on him next time, and no coat.'

'No coat?'

'Unless it's cold, of course. And if he does come in a coat, can his dad remove it before he comes into this room?'

'Yes, well I suppose that would be better.' She then left with Sebastian, who was beaming like a person who thinks they have dodged a bullet.

**

Trevor was a very different kettle of fish. Same day, same age, same vaccinations, another town.

I called his name in the waiting room and saw a Hell's Angel rise from the seat and walk towards me. He had muscles up to his ears, tattoos on his face, and a shaven head. Me? Scared? Don't be ridiculous. Oh, and he had his four-year-old son behind him with spiky hair, in a tracksuit, all clean and shiny.

'Hello, Trevor,' I said in my kindest voice, trying not to show my fear. If I hurt this little boy, what would his father do to me?

'Say hello, Trevor,' his father demanded as they sat down in my office.

'No!'

Here we go again, I thought. 'It's all right,' I said, 'he doesn't have to.' I quickly went through the formalities, and all seemed above board. 'And you're dad?'

'Who else would I be?'

'Sorry to ask, but we get boyfriends of mums, uncles, grand-fathers — not that you look old enough to be a grandfather,' I quickly corrected. Dad just looked at me. 'Yes. I'll just get the injections ready if you would take Trevor's top off.'

I prepared the injections with my back to father and son; a trick I used with this age group, putting myself between them and what I was doing. 'Ready?' I turned around and Trevor was now on his dad's knee, arm held firmly. That kid was going nowhere. I did injection one, and Trevor screamed.

'Just turn him around and I'll do the other injection,' I shouted over the noise. Dad nodded, did a very nifty about-turn on his son, and I did the deed. High fives all round — well, not quite. Trevor escaped from his dad's grip and yelled 'I fucking hate you,' before making a bid for freedom. I'm not sure who he was swearing at.

Dad got up to go after him. 'I'll bring the red book out to you,' I called to the back of his jacket with the bloody skull on it.

Once I had done the paperwork, I peeped outside into the waiting room to see if they were still there, which they were. 'Okay now?' I asked as I handed the book over.

'He's fine, nurse.' They got up to leave. 'Come on, you little git, I'll buy you a Big Mac,' his dad said as they walked down the corridor.

So completely different in attitude. So completely different in technique. But ask me which I prefer? Yes, you're correct, the Hell's Angel and his little git.

As for Sebastian, Dad did bring him back. He still put up a fight, and his dad was about as much use as a chocolate fireguard, but did I care? No. I was on holiday.

Chapter 32

Make my day!

I was used to drama. Screaming, crying, fainting, vomiting — or even worse, not screaming when a child stopped breathing, or breath-holding, as we liked to call it. But I drew the line at drunken, abusive adults. No, it wasn't a parent in my clinic— in fact, it had nothing to do with me — but I had to go and stick my big nose in, didn't I.

It was a normal day at the coalface, and this morning my clinic was in a room just outside the treatment rooms at a large health center, so slightly more noisy than usual. That apart, it had been a good session with everything running smoothly. I had one more child to see, and then I was off for the rest of the day, so I was feeling good about the world.

Then we heard a kerfuffle outside. I was answering a young mum's worried questions about the vaccines I was about to pop into her one-year-old when I heard shouting and swearing outside my door. My colleague said she would go and see what all the fuss was about while I carried on talking to the mum. She was back in a flash and told us that a madman was running wild in the building and threatening staff, and that the police had been called.

'A madman?'

'Well, he's drunk.'

'Drunk?'

'Or on drugs. His girlfriend is in the treatment room and the staff have locked the door, which he's not happy about.'

'How did you find all this out? You were only gone a minute.'

'Sylvia.'

'Ah.' Sylvia was one of the receptionists at the practice and had relayed all this to my colleague in ten seconds flat, while the 'madman' had ventured off to find another way to get to his partner.

'Oh well, he's gone now,' I said, and picked up my conversation with the baby's mother — 'LET ME THE FUCK IN!'

'Oh, for goodness sake.' I got up to go and see who this person was who was upsetting my clinic.

'Don't go out there,' warned my colleague. Too late. I shut the door behind me to be confronted by a weed of a man, about 5 feet 2 inches tall and wobbling alarmingly. He looked at me. 'WHAT?' he shouted.

'Will you please keep your foul mouth shut and go away?'

He took a step towards me. 'Why should I do that? I'm going in there and I'm getting my woman.'

'I don't think so.'

'Oh, right. And who's going to stop me?'

'Me!' I stood between him and the treatment-room door, crossed my arms and stared him down. I should point out that I was at this time of my life physically fit, I am 5 feet 8 inches tall, and I happened to have 3-inch heels on that day, so I towered above him. And did I mention I also did martial arts?

He took a few steps back, looking quite bewildered, and had just opened his mouth to make some sort of comeback when one of the male GPs came around the corner. 'What's going on here, then?'

'You okay, mate?' asked the man, his attitude changing completely on meeting another male.

'I'm fine. You come and sit in the waiting room like a good chap, and I'll try and sort all this out. Okay?'

'Yep. Good. Okay.'

The doctor led him away and I went back to what I was doing, only to find two open-mouthed people looking at me. 'Are you okay?' asked the mum.

'You shouldn't have done that,' said my colleague. 'He might have hurt you.'

'Nah. if I'd given him a slight push he would have fallen over.' As I said this, I saw the person in question being led away by the police in handcuffs.

Two days later I received a phone call from my manager. 'Carol, I believe you were involved in an incident at the clinic on Tuesday morning?'

'What? Oh yes, that. It was nothing.' Here we go, I thought, commendation, bravery medal, interview with the press.

'What were you thinking? You could have been seriously hurt!'

'No, I couldn't. It was more likely that he would have been hurt. One jab to his knee with my heels and he would have been down on the floor pleading for mercy,' I replied, trying to lighten the mood.

'That's even worse! You might have injured him, and then the trust would have been sued.'

'What? Seriously?'

'Just count your blessings that it ended the way it did. Now, I think you need to do a "Dealing with Conflict in the Work Environment" course, and we will say no more about it.' She rang off, leaving me staring at a silent phone with my mouth open.

Two months later I turned up for my naughty-girl course at a local hospital with fourteen other naughty people. We had coffee and waited, and waited for our trainer to arrive only to be told an hour later that the course was cancelled due to unforeseen circumstances, and would be rescheduled for a later date.

We never did do the course. The rumour was that the instructor had been sacked for aggressive behaviour to a colleague, but we never found out if it were true or not.

Chapter 33

Wet, wet, wet!

Occasionally I was asked to work with student nurses who were doing their community rotation. The way nurses were being trained now was completely beyond my comprehension, but I did know they were with me only to observe, and under no circumstances allowed to do something. Oh, how things had changed!

It was a hot August day, and I was in a room at the top of a health center which was stuffy in summer and cold in winter, and today it had an extra body in there to bring the temperature up even further.

That student nurse in question was keen to learn and I had already talked her through the immunisation schedule, gone briefly over the diseases we were trying to prevent, and talked about common side effects. Today was a practical demonstration of what she had learned so far.

All went according to plan though we did have a high rate of DNAs (did not attends) that day, which was unfortunate but normal for that practice. We got a good rate of parents attending with their babies but this fell away at the twelve-month appointment, and the uptake rate got even worse for the pre-school boosters.

I gave the student the job of going into the waiting room and calling the next person in, and then under my supervision, she did all the pre-vaccination checks and explained to the parent what we were doing and why. I filled in where necessary and asked the person who had brought the baby if they had any questions. Then I did the injection and the paperwork.

The first problem we encountered that day was a one-year-old who came with her dad — or was he? After going through the normal line of questioning I asked, 'And are you dad?'

'Yes. Well, sort of.'

Alarm bells started ringing. 'Sort of?'

'Yes, I'm her mum's partner.'

'But you're not married to mum, and you've not adopted the baby?'

'No. Does it make a difference?'

'Legally, yes. Is there any way I can get in touch with her mum on the phone?'

'No, she's got a hospital appointment. She'll have her phone switched off.'

'How about her biological father? Does he still have access?'

'He's in prison.'

'Right. And mum didn't give you any written authorisation for you to bring baby today?'

'How would we know that?'

I took the appointment letter from him and pointed out the bold print at the bottom asking for this, in the event that the legal parent or guardian could not attend with the child.

'Oh. Right. We didn't see that.'

'Sorry for the inconvenience, but she'll have to come back. I have no legal authority to do this today.'

'But that's ridiculous.'

'It's also the law.'

I felt for him, I did really. People bringing infants and young children for their vaccinations without the proper authority happens all too frequently, and my hands were tied. Had I known the family dynamics, as the health visitors do, it could have been a different matter, but I did so many clinics I couldn't possibly know who was shacked up with whom, which child's father was which, and that grandma always brought the little ones, or they would never have got their injections. It was a minefield.

We didn't want these complications. We wanted to vaccinate these tiny people so that they would be safe, but what with litigation and the issues that some people had over vaccines and their possible effects, it was more than my job was worth to go against the tide.

The next appointment was a sixteen-week old baby with his mum, attending for his third set of injections. Mum was nervous and I made sure the student did everything correctly as I gulped down a glass of water, then refilled it and put it on the desk.

I gave the first injection and the baby cried, and then asked mum to turn her child around so that I could do the second. As this was done the baby took in a large breath but didn't breathe out. He didn't cry, just lay in his mother's arms going a little grey. 'What's happening?' The mother looked terrified, and why wouldn't she? I had just injected her baby twice, and now he wasn't breathing.

'It's okay,' I said, with a calmness in my voice that wasn't in my head, 'it's just breath-holding.' I leaned in close to the child and blew gently into his face. Nothing. 'The water, the glass of water,' I said to the student, who also seemed to be holding her breath.

It all happened in slow motion. The girl picked up the full tumbler of water and threw it all over the baby and his mother.

It worked, of course. The baby started screaming and mother stopped breathing and shivered as the water dripped off her chin and onto her soaked top. 'Whoops, sorry,' said the student as she grabbed a heap of paper towels to dab some of the water damage from the mother and child.

What I was going to do before Watergate was sprinkle a few drops of water onto the child's face. If that hadn't done the trick, he would have gone into a faint and then everything would have gone back to normal, but it is even more scary to see a small infant collapse in your arms' so I was trying to prevent that, which we did. Though I could just see the incident form, 'Baby needed resuscitating from drowning.' That would have taken some explaining!

Chapter 34

This orange is dead!

The incident with the student nurse actually did me a good turn. She fed back to her tutor about her experience and how I had handled the unscheduled christening of the baby and his mother. This in turn got back to the powers that be, and the next stage of my career started to form.

We had an acute shortage of immunisation trainers in the trust where I worked.

This was due to yet another round of reorganisation and new guidelines on how immunisers should be trained.

It meant taking the current group of trainers away from their day jobs for longer periods, and, due to the reorganisation, this was proving more and more difficult for them.

When I was asked if I would like to do a three-day training course called 'Train the Trainer' (well, that was to the point) I jumped at the chance, especially as one of the people recommending me was my line manager, which meant she would allow me to do the job for which they were training me.

There were ten of us, and apart from myself and one other staff nurse, the others were all health visitors from different areas around the county. The idea was that the trainer wouldn't have to travel far to teach on her patch, which would be more practical for her and her attendees. It would also save travel expenses for the trust, though this was never given as a reason for the selection of students for this course.

A lot of what we covered I had already done in Manchester, so it acted as a refresher and brought me up to date with current research. It was the teaching methods that I had to get my mind around; how to engage twenty people on regular updates when they probably didn't want to be there, thought it a waste of time, and would tell you that they could do the job better than the person teaching them.

The training of staff who, although qualified nurses, had never actually done immunisations before, was to be a two-day course (not the half-day that I got). Even though there was a huge amount of information to get through, set out by The Health Protection Agency, I had no doubt that they would be willing participants, if they had the same mindset as I had when I did this training.

One of the tasks set for our final day's training was to do a ten-minute PowerPoint presentation on a subject that had been given to us on the first day of the course. This was a problem for me as I had never produced a PowerPoint presentation and didn't know where to start.

Enter, him indoors. Being at management level, he had to do this sort of thing all the time, and helped me to put mine together.

My topic was pandemic flu. I knew very little about this to begin with, but when I did some research I found the whole subject fascinating and frightening in equal measures. I also found keeping my talk down to ten minutes was going to be difficult. Before my search on Google for facts and figures on this subject, I was wondering how on earth I would fill the allotted time.

All the presentations were very good, and I was second from last. I started with a slight wobble to my voice, but three minutes into my topic I was totally immersed in the subject and thoroughly enjoying myself. I got a round of applause at the end, which I wasn't expecting, and felt relieved and pleased as I sat down.

But the buzz I got from the process stayed with me for days. This was what I was meant to do. Finally, I'd found my true vocation.

***

As with many things in the NHS, the strategic plan to train our staff didn't work. It wasn't for want of trying, but the health visitors on the course found it almost impossible to get time to deliver the training, due to the increasing demands within their roles. It became clear early in the game that this job was going to be down to myself and the immunisation co-ordinator for the trust, and no one else.

We often worked together and got on well. Jane gave me more and more responsibilities and we even produced our own training slides, something which I now loved doing, after making up packs with all the HPA handouts for reading at home.

It was an impossible task to go through every single power point without sending our students into a coma. I tried to bring humour into the training with cartoon characters floating onto slides, and silly photos, and Jane devised games to stimulate teamwork and discussion.

When it came to the practical work, we took our fair share of oranges in, so that nurses could practise the different techniques for the administration of the vaccines. I did find one male student stabbing his orange with the cry of 'Die, die you bastard!' I relieved him of his victim and told him to go and get a coffee. I think it had all been too much for him.

But the feedback was good and 97% of people on our courses said that they had had a good learning experience, so we were getting something right.

Chapter 35

Don't leave me this way

Life was hectic. For a short while I was doing three jobs for the trust; my 16 hours a week as an immunisations nurse, 6-8 hours each week as a stop smoking advisor, and bank work for the training department, which averaged about 12 hours each month.

I was also having issues with my back. All the bending and crouching to get to little legs was harming my spine, and it all came tumbling down one day. Literally.

I was doing a monthly clinic at a GP surgery when I had a problem. At this clinic I would go into the waiting room and call each child in as per their appointment time. The staff at the practice left me to it except for a nice cup of tea, which they brought to me if they got time.

It was the next to last appointment, and I was in a bad way. I had already phoned my physio and made an appointment with her for the next evening after work. I had just done the second injection on a 16-week old baby when I felt something go in my back, and sat down on the floor.

'Are you all right?' asked the mum of the baby.

'No,' I moaned. 'I don't think I can get up.'

'Oh dear,' she replied, and left the room; to get help, I presumed. Wrong! I sat there impatiently, in pain, waiting for somebody to come and help me.

Eventually there was a gentle tap at the door, 'Carol?' A face peeped into the room. 'Carol! What are you doing down there?'

'I can't get up,' I gasped.

'Just a mo.' She disappeared and returned with another member of staff, and together they got me on a chair. 'We wondered where you were when you didn't come out for the last patient.'

'Didn't the woman that was in here tell you I needed help?'

'No, she just left.'

'Great,' I said, as shooting pains travelled up and down my leg with increasing sharpness.

I ended up being off work for six weeks, and even when I was well enough to be in the office, my ability to carry on immunising was in doubt.

I visited a neurologist during my sick leave, after an x-ray showed osteoarthritis of the lumbar spine, and his advice was to retire. When I said that this wasn't possible, he replied, 'So change your job then, because you can't go back to what you were doing.'

Luckily for me I had two very understanding managers at this time. Yes, another reshuffle had seen my old manager go on to bigger and better things, and she was replaced by not one new manager, but two.

After a great deal of consultation with the health and safety bods, moving and handling experts, and reading my consultant's notes, it was decided that it would no longer be safe for me to immunise and that they would find me another suitable role instead.

'Like what?' I asked.

'No idea,' came their honest reply.

Once again fate took charge, this time in the guise of an influenza pandemic as swine flu spread across the planet.

Chapter 36

Atishoo, atishoo, we all get overtime!

It had to happen; it was only a matter of time. We had our first flu pandemic for forty years, but this time we were ready. A vaccine was constructed very quickly, and antivirals were produced by the lorry-load.

As for my part, I got a short-term full-time contract with Jane, working on all things flu-related.

One of our first jobs was to train as many people in the trust as we could to give flu vaccines. This ranged from HCAs (health care assistants) to consultants and senior managers. Once that little task was done, we had to vaccinate as many frontline staff as possible.

If the whole country was going to go down with flu, we had to have a workforce who wouldn't get the virus themselves. As a trust we had taken the controversial decision before this pandemic to train HCAs in the administration of flu vaccines, so we already a had a willing and able workforce who could do this job.

Some saw the HCA training as a very good idea, others as the thin end of the wedge; the slippery slope, taking a job away from trained nurses and undermining their years of training and experience. It was seen by the GPs as a cheap way to deliver this service, thus getting more money into their business, and at the time of swine flu, a godsend to the health protection team.

***

I was one of the first people in our county to get the swine flu vaccine. Did I worry because it had been mass-produced very quickly? No. Did I worry about the constituents of the vaccine?

No. Did I worry about the side-effects of the vaccine? No. Did I worry about coming down with a possible killer flu? YES! To be truthful, any flu virus has the potential to kill, but this was taken more seriously by WHO, and so it should be.

The attitude of some NHS staff mystified me. They flatly refused to consider being vaccinated, though they could very easily spread the virus to their families, and more to the point, given their line of work, to sick and vulnerable patients.

Saying all this, we met ourselves coming back as a small team of immunisers travelled all over the area setting up clinics to offer this vaccine and the seasonal flu vaccine to all frontline staff.

The worst case of fear I'd ever seen was at one of the major hospitals in the area, when all the staff from the dental department came along to get the little prick. The last in line was a consultant dental surgeon. When he came into our room he had beads of sweat on his brow and looked very pale indeed.

'Are you all right?' I asked, as he sat shaking on the chair.

'I hate needles,' he said in a quiet voice.

'Well done for turning up, then,' I congratulated him as I stuck the needle in his arm.

'Just get on with it, the sooner it's over the better.'

'I've done it. Now go to the other nurse for the seasonal vaccine.'

He looked at me as if I had two heads. 'I didn't feel a thing.' A smile appeared on his face, and his colour had returned to normal. He trotted over to my colleague, who jabbed him in the other arm, and off he went, as happy as Larry.

We did get the odd faint, but not many. The one that remains with me was the tattooed male nurse. He worked in mental health and I assumed his manager didn't mind the array of artwork inked into his skin. He also had a lot of body piercings, and they were just the ones I could see.

'Will it hurt?' he asked.

'Not much, but your arm will be sore tomorrow.'

'I don't like needles,' he confessed as he rolled his sleeve up, very slowly.

'You're joking. What about all this?' I waved my arm around his body as if I were trying to put a spell on him.

'Different.'

'Still a needle.'

'But I want these. They are works of art.'

'So is my work, mate,' I said as I searched for a bit of bicep that wasn't covered with ink. 'Here.' I found my spot and injected the vaccine before my eyes started seeing double again. 'All done. Wasn't that bad, was it?' As I said this the tattooed man slid gracefully to the floor in a dead faint. I just managed to protect his head from hitting any hard surfaces before he completely bottomed out.

He was fine fifteen minutes later and feeling somewhat embarrassed that he had been such a wimp. He promised to come back the following week for his second vaccine, but I didn't see him again. Still, one out of two ain't bad.

***

We ran other clinics that offered an egg-free swine-flu vaccine. This was for people who had severe egg allergies and couldn't have the normal flu vaccine, as these are grown on hen's eggs (now there are egg-free seasonal vaccines available). This vaccine was in short supply, and because we wanted to make sure that the right people got them, we did a community clinic in each area. The group we were trying to protect had underlying health problems to start with, so they didn't need the flu as well. Patients were referred to us mostly by their GPs, and some by their consultants. One child was brought in by his father, who didn't seem to have a handle on his son's condition at all. 'He has a bad heart,' he told us, 'and he can't eat eggs.'

'Does he react to eggs?' I asked

'I think so. He doesn't like them.'

'Not liking them isn't the same as being allergic to them,' I pointed out.

Dad just shrugged. 'All I know is his consultant said he's to have this egg-free one and the other as well.'

'Which other?'

'The normal one. The one he gets every year on account of his bad heart.'

'The seasonal flu vaccine?'

'Yep. That one.'

Now I was confused. 'But the seasonal flu vaccine has egg protein in it.'

More shrugging of the shoulders.

'I think I'd better try and speak to his specialist.' This took ages, and when I did get through to the hospital's paediatric department, my patient's consultant was away for the day.

I did get to speak to another specialist, however. 'I'll just access his notes,' she said, and I heard keys being punched. 'Ah yes. Dad's quite right. Both the egg-free swine flu and the seasonal

flu vaccines have been requested.'

'But the seasonal flu vaccine has egg protein in it.'

'Does it?'

'Yes.'

'Well, I'm only telling you what it says here.'

'Okay. I'll give him the egg-free vaccine, but we don't carry the seasonal flu vaccine at these clinics, so he'll have to see his GP next week for that.'

'Why not?'

'Because they have egg in them.' I felt as if I was trying to explain how nice meat was to a vegetarian.

'But he can't have two vaccines that close together. If it isn't today, he will have to wait four weeks.'

I had to sit down. 'No,' I said slowly, 'that only applies to live vaccines. Flu vaccines are not live.'

'Are you sure?'

'Yes. You may want to read the chapter in the green book. You might find some clarity there.' She didn't reply, just put the phone down on me.

Later that day, when we were driving home, I brought the subject up with Jane. 'I think we need to do some training with doctors.'

'We've tried, you know we have. They think it's beneath them. But after what you've told me, I do need to have a conversation with the manager at that hospital.'

I was very tired, and I did wonder at that moment if I had been talking to a consultant at all.

Maybe it was just some passing stranger who thought it would save time if they answered the phone. Why bother these busy doctors?

Chapter 37

Now, that's what I call a vaccine!

The wonders of modern science. A vaccine that could prevent cancer. Amazing!

This was the advent of the HPV, given to girls at secondary school to prevent cervical cancer, and once again, I was in at the start of this game-changer.

The NHS did a massive publicity campaign, school health got all geared up to deliver the vaccine, and extra staff were recruited to help with the program. As these vaccines were given to young adults and they could sit in a chair next to the vaccinator I was more than willing to participate in this; after all, giving the flu vaccine had not had a detrimental effect on my back problems.

There were issues over consent; parents felt nervous about a new vaccine being given to their child, and rumours of awful side-effects spread through social media, but thankfully most parents were as blown away as we were. A vaccine to stop cancer!

One known side-effect was very occasionally dizziness and fainting. I felt that it was no more prevalent with this vaccine than any other, and hysteria had a part to play, just as it had with the BCG.

The first school clinic I helped with had its fair share of panicky schoolgirls, which wasn't helped by one of the school health team telling the recipient of the vaccine that they might feel dizzy or faint, which they then promptly did. After the first session we had seven girls lying in a quiet area with their legs on elevated on chairs. That was until sanity in the form of a male teacher appeared. 'What's going on here?'

'We feel sick, sir, and dizzy.'

'Rubbish. Get up and get back to class.' He turned and left, and so did the seven girls. I liked that teacher. I did suggest we took him to all our clinics, but apparently that wouldn't have been acceptable.

At another school, we had the girl with the panic attack. When she came to me she was already hyperventilating. After trying unsuccessfully to bring her breathing back to normal I told her to go and breathe into a paper bag; old-fashioned, but it usually works. Not in this case, unfortunately.

Next time I looked up from my task the girl had three members of the school health team around her, and she was getting worse. Her mother was called for, and as she walked into the hall to collect her daughter she looked skywards. 'Not again.'

Shortly afterwards an ambulance arrived, and mum and daughter were whisked off to A&E. 'She does this all the time,' a teacher told us later. 'She is always in A&E. It's becoming a real problem.'

I shouldn't have been so flippant, and I never was again. Panic attacks are awful, and the person going through them thinks they are about to die, but I had never seen such an extreme case, and have never witnessed one since.

The schedule and the vaccine for the HPV have changed over the years, but it is proving to be a brilliant vaccine, and we will see fewer deaths from this awful disease in years to come. Here's to the heroes who promoted the program and gave the vaccines, but mostly to the girls that had the vaccine all those years ago; you were trailblazers.

Chapter 38

Just sniff this up

'Do you think it's a good idea to teach children to inhale chemical substances up their noses?'

As no one laughed I decided to shut up. After all, these were all the top bods from the Department of Health, and I was lower than whale shit among such elevated people.

We were talking about nasal flu vaccine for children, the next big thing in our fight for health and wellbeing for the population of England.

It was good — it was very good — and trials had shown that the way it worked it would be effective without many side-effects. The only chink in its armour was that it didn't have a very long shelf life because it was a live vaccine. This could be another problem, but only if we let it.

Why, you might ask, do we need to vaccinate children against a disease that usually doesn't make them that ill? Good question, considering that kids aren't often poorly with the flu virus. In fact, sometimes we don't even know that they have had flu because they will only be off colour and off school for a few days, and then they are as right as rain.

But here's the thing. They might seem okay, they might act okay, but they are still infectious! I kid you not. Surprised? Well, you should be. I was when I found out, and as we all know, children, especially tiny ones, are bioterrorists, gladly giving away snotty kisses, sticking fingers up noses and other places I don't even want to think about, and then sharing.

'Why should my child be exposed to yet another unnecessary vaccine?' asked one belligerent mum, when we did some research into what children and their parents thought about flu protection being added to the UK routine immunisation schedule.

'To help protect themselves, their families and people who are vulnerable due to poor health,'came the reply.

'I thought people with health issues could get the flu vaccine anyway, so I ask again, why should my child be a guinea pig for a new vaccine? Surely it's their responsibility to get the jab and protect themselves.'

'Yes, but people with a poor immune system don't always get full cover from the vaccine; they can still get flu in some instances.' Good reply, but it wasn't making any difference to this lady. She had made her mind up.

The idea was to eventually give the vaccine to all 2-18 year old childen, thus taking out at one go a whole group of the population who might spread the virus, and make flu season less hazardous for the rest of us.

It was however, going to be a logistical nightmare, and pilot schemes were planned in various areas, all with slightly different ways of getting the vaccine from the fridge to the nasal passages. We would start with 4-11 year old children. The whole age group would take a few years to get to, realistically.

In our area we had a three-prong approach:

1). Going to the GP.

2). Going to a community clinic.

3). Going into a chemist and letting the pharmacists do the deed.

Number 3, I thought, was a touch of genius, but that remained to be seen.

To do all this, the Department of Health put extra funding into these 'let's try it and see' health trusts, to pay for extra staff, fridges, training, and so on. I was promoted on a short contract to be the co-coordinator for all this in my area. I took part in the recruitment of extra staff, and the training of any staff involved, and I was going to head up some clinics and be a general troubleshooter, but then disaster struck.

Him indoors and I were having a short break in Edinburgh in mid-August, and very nice it was too. As I was going to be a bit busy for the next four months, I saw it as my last chance that year to relax.

We had just gone into a shoe shop because the lace on one of my husband's boots had snapped. He went upstairs to the men's department, leaving me to take a seat in the ladies' department, and that's when it happened. I was half-sitting, half-standing when I saw, in my peripheral vision, the most beautiful pair of shoes. I twisted and tried to stand up again, all in one movement. It didn't work. A tearing pain ripped through my lower back, which saw me sit down with a thud and I cried out in agony.

At this point my beloved came down, chuntering about the shop not having laces for the boots they sold, which was in his opinion ridiculous. He glanced in my direction. 'Come on then,' he said, and went outside. I swear he'd gone ten yards before he realised I wasn't in his wake. He popped his head around the door. 'I hope you're not waiting to try some shoes on,' he said, joking, and then he saw my face.

'I can't move,' I whimpered.

Now my hubby was once a Boy Scout and 'be prepared,' had never really left his psyche. Having once been floored by acute back pain himself, he now always carried strong painkillers with him. He produced these, the shop staff produced some water and I inspected the wrapper the tablets were cocooned in. It looked a bit suspect to me — God alone knew how long they had been lurking in his wallet — but hell, I was in pain, so I downed them.

After about fifteen minutes the pain did seem to ease, enough at any rate for me to get up, get out of the shop and get into a taxi. After a nice sleep I felt much better and put the terrible pain down to a muscle spasm. I even managed to get out for dinner, though I didn't hang around for pudding.

Home the next day and then back into work on Monday. No, that didn't happen. Over the next few days the pain just got worse and worse. I could hardly walk. I was off sick for the next eight weeks, the busiest time of the whole pilot, and all I could do was phone in to the weekly team meeting, make any phone calls that needed doing from our end, and do a bit of data capture. I missed the main event and was truly fed up.

I did manage to observe one community clinic thanks to him indoors. It was in a rural area, and he was my chauffeur and helper for the day. I watched several children have the vaccine administered, saw how they reacted, watched the interaction and methodology of the staff, and then went into the waiting room to observe how our survey was going.

We had devised two different survey sheets. One was for the very young and had lots of pictures on it. With the help of their parents they ticked some boxes on the paper and then got a badge and sweets for their time. The second sheet was intended for the 8-11-year age group, and was supposed to be simple enough for that group to fill in alone.

One young man of about eight seemed to be having some trouble, and I offered my help. 'Do you need a hand?'

He looked me up and down with contempt. 'I'm not stupid, you know,' he said, and then got back to considering his answers. Well, that told me.

Once back at work I did some mopping-up. I attended some meetings for Jane, who had run the whole shebang without me, and did more work on the so-important data for the Department of Health.

The uptake wasn't brilliant, but no one ever thought it would be. For many of the pilot areas, it was the same story. We had proved that it could be done, and how it would be done was yet to be ironed out. It wouldn't be long before it would be expected by parents, especially when they saw that their children didn't mind the mist being given nasally — it just tickled — and that there were just a few minor side effects.

This sadly would be my swansong, both for my immunisation career and my nursing career.

After an attempt at going back to work full-time in 2014 my back condition just got worse, resulting in surgery and my retirement.

I wasn't happy. I had been forced to leave a job I loved, a job where I felt I had made a difference. But sometimes you must face the fact that you've done your bit, and move over for the next generation to carry on where you left off.

Is it just a coincidence that the immunisation rates have dropped considerably since I retired and Jane went off to pastures new! Of course. However, we did work incredibly hard to improve the immunisation uptake in our county, and managed to see the MMR rate reach 95% during our watch. We went out of our way, went out of our comfort zone, and went where no immuniser had been before. We worked silly hours, many of which we didn't even expect to get paid for, and we got results.

Why? Because we believed in what we were doing. Because we wanted to stop killer diseases coming back — and they will if we don't get the cover up to 95% again. But mostly because we loved the job.

We were not a two-woman band. We were part of a bigger team, but not that much bigger, and they will now carry on that vital work without us.

I shouldn't say this, but I will anyway. I still feel we did it better. Me and Jane were the A-Team, though sometimes I think we were more like Bugs Bunny and the Road Runner. I have seen many changes in the NHS over 50 years, some good, some not so good.

I hated the matriarchal figure which terrorised the nursing staff and many doctors when I first went into nursing, but they ran the hospital like a well-oiled machine, and the new Modern Matron doesn't, because the old figurehead ran the entire hospital, not just a department.

When each ward had dedicated cleaners it sparkled, they took pride in their work, and it might be my age getting the facts wrong, but did we have as many hospital acquired infections then as now?

People didn't question their treatment way back then, which was a bad thing. I'm all for patients involvement and knowledge is power. The patient should be the person who, after all the information is given to them that make the decision about their treatment. As medical staff we may not like or agree with that decision, but we do have to respect it.

And as for immunisations well where do I start?

Such massive advances have been made just in my lifetime and because of this millions of lives are now saved every year worldwide.

There are two things that have contributed to better health on our planet more than anything else. Those two things are clean water and immunisations.

I feel, that in a very small way I helped in the second of those two innovations, and hopefully at some level helped to save some lives, and as a by-product, met and worked with fantastic people. Thanks to you all for making my life so much richer.

But for the time being, 'That's all, folks!'

Also by the same author

Steph Taylor has a black belt for relationships and is a third Dan in the art of getting involved. But, why has this middle-aged woman retired at such an early age? What has caused her PTSD? And how did she get mixed up with a suicidal woman? Are the police really going to arrest her?

Read this rollercoaster tale according to the word of Steph, where she looks at her life now, and retrospectively, in this hilarious tale of modern-day family.

I'LL NEVER BE A
NINJA
NOW!

CAROL BISSETT

Paperback: 181 pages
ISBN-13: 978-1916021761

Sally thinks she has escaped her sordid past, but it's catching up with her far too quickly.

Richard feels he is being punished by being posted to Cumbria, a far cry from the London Met.

Why do Dawn and son, Alex, have such a tense relationship? Emma thinks there is more to their issues, and confides in opinion with her friends, Oliver and Tristan. But they have problems of their own!

All so different. But one thing binds them together, the place where they live, the Manor.

Paperback: 194 pages
ISBN-13: 978-1999615635

Born on the other side of the world Carol Bissett has always been a writer. Now living back in Cheshire after 23 years in Cumbria she is concentrating on her writing for the first time.

Carol now lives in Warrington with her husband of 46 years and still has two sons at home.

Lightning Source UK Ltd.
Milton Keynes UK
UKHW010630171020
371758UK00001B/99